"Loren Sandford has done it again. *The Prophetic Church* is heart-gripping, bold, insightful, innovative and convicting. Every prophetically gifted individual needs to read and live with the attitude and in the spiritual atmosphere described in this book. With wisdom, Loren Sandford not only defines what it takes to have a healthy prophetic community, but how prophetically gifted individuals should live in the community of the Church, and in so doing have a long and vibrant ministry."

—**John Paul Jackson**, founder,
Streams Ministries International

"Loren Sandford pleads for a deep and intimate relationship with God in a secular society caught in an out-of-control downward spiral. Loren calls us to seek first the Kingdom of God and lifts up a vision of lighthouse churches to show the way Home."

—**John Arnott**, founding pastor,
Toronto Airport Christian Fellowship

"Loren Sandford has written a book about making the journey in the Spirit to the place where the Kingdom provides the environment for real Church to emerge. It is an honest book about coming out of a sterile past into a vibrant future. Loren is building a people who can receive under pressure and prosper in the heat of battle—a community of passion that worships wholeheartedly and prays like a bride, not a widow.

"It takes time, faith and patience, and only people who have sought the Lord and been found by Him can do it. Most churches want to get into a high place in God. Sadly, many of them dream about the outcome but fail to understand the process that takes them there. It is the process that makes us rich. How we travel is as important as reaching our destination. This is a book for travelers, not tourists."

—**Graham Cooke**, author,
Approaching the Heart of Prophecy

"Loren Sandford is great example of the kind of leader we need for a move of the Spirit that, along with other distinctives, would combine a love for the written Word of God with a love for the presence and power of God. His deep appreciation for the Bible, along with his passion for the presence, power and leading of the Holy Spirit, provide us with a great example. *The Prophetic Church* will prove a valuable tool in helping the 'both/and' Church to emerge. Loren engages us with a passion for the Person of God, yet he calls us to be people who fulfill the purposes of God for this *kairos* (chosen) time."

—**Marc Dupont**, Mantle of Praise Ministries, Inc.

"This interesting, well-written, intensely practical and sometimes provocative book by Loren Sandford confronts the Church of Jesus Christ that he loves and has served faithfully for more than thirty years as a pastor and prophet to wake up to her mandate. The mandate is to be known by her love (see John 13:35).

"In this treatise, Loren builds an airtight prophetic case that love, not power, is the primary mark of the Spirit-filled Christian and community. He challenges us to move forward to take our places as the true light in the desperately reeling world community that Jesus states we are.

"Bless you, Loren, my long-time friend and always challenging confidante, for your prophetic and pastoral heart."

—**Fred Wright**, international coordinator, Partners in Harvest; author, *The World's Greatest Revivals*

THE
PROPHETIC
CHURCH

THE
PROPHETIC
CHURCH

WIELDING *the* POWER
to CHANGE *the* WORLD

R. LOREN SANDFORD

Chosen
a division of Baker Publishing Group
Grand Rapids, Michigan

Published by Chosen Books
A division of Baker Publishing Group
P.O. Box 6287, Grand Rapids, MI 49516–6287
www.chosenbooks.com

Printed in the United States of America

Library of Congress Cataloging-in-Publication Data
Sandford, R. Loren.
    The prophetic church : wielding the power to change the world / R. Loren
Sandford.
        p.   cm.
    ISBN 978-0-8007-9462-0 (pbk.)
    1. Church renewal. 2. Revivals. 3. Christianity—Forecasting. 4. End of the
world. I. Title
BV600.3.S26 2008
269—dc22   2008038062

Unless otherwise indicated, Scripture is taken from the New American Standard Bible®, Copyright © 1960, 1962, 1963, 1968, 1971, 1972, 1973, 1975, 1977, 1995 by The Lockman Foundation. Used by permission.

Contents

Contents

Acknowledgments

Kris Vallotton, for his teaching and books inspiring me to go deeper into an awareness of our royal identity as believers.

Danny Silk, whose teaching gave me new language for the culture of honor I have worked for in the Church all my life.

Lance Wallnau, for a conference teaching that alerted me to the concept of oneness as a force multiplier.

My son and ministry partner, Nathan, from whom I borrowed the concept of the forgotten ones, the mediocre ones and the great ones.

My parents, John and Paula Sandford, without whose influence and inspiration I would be doing nothing in ministry that I am doing today.

PART I

COMMUNITY

1

Islands of Glory in a Sea of Mud

I offer this book having been inspired by a strong prophetic sense concerning the future of the Church in the Western world. Revival is surely coming and will touch many thousands through churches and ministries willing to receive it, but bluntly stated, I do not believe we will see sweeping culture-changing revival in North America and the Western world despite the prayers of those of us who understand the need and desperately long for God to send it. Bad news for the culture, but good news for God's people! Both Matthew 24 and the Revelation to John present an end-time scenario preceding the Lord's return in which the world system continues its chosen path to destruction while the Church enjoys a golden age of harvest, even under persecution.

Two key factors play into this assessment of the state of the culture of the Western world and its prospects for revival. First, a great many of us asked for revival and God lovingly sent it, but when He did, we turned it down because we objected to the way it looked. This is how it happened. In 1994 He poured out His power on what was then the Toronto Airport Vineyard Christian Fellowship and is now the Toronto Airport Christian Fellowship. The impact of that outpouring has echoed worldwide and produced enormous fruit for the Kingdom of God. Again in 1996 He lit the fire at Brownsville Assembly of God in Pensacola, Florida. Once more the ripples spread far and wide. Across the country similar lights sprang up in places like Smithton, Missouri and Harvest Rock Church in Pasadena, California, for example. There were many others.

Each of these venues saw unusual manifestations of the power and presence of God. People laughed, fell out in the Spirit, shook, roared and more. The Holy Spirit changed, refreshed and renewed untold thousands of lives. We saw healings and miracles. Many received inspiration to go to the mission field, where thousands upon thousands have been healed, delivered and even raised from the dead.

As the years passed following these outpourings, the North American Church in general gradually but surely turned it all down. Too messy! Too out of control! Pastor after pastor and church after church opted for less disturbing forms of church life and invited the Holy Spirit to tone it down, desiring that the Lion of Judah should behave in a more "tame" and orderly manner. As the life inevitably ebbed from our churches and spiritual lives, we began to cry out to God once more to send revival, but His answer has been, "I already sent revival, but you didn't like it!"

A significant remnant has been crying out in repentance for this rejection of the gift of God, praying that God would cause the lightning to strike once more. God has been preparing pockets of hungry saints to receive. He has given us tools for ministry in inner healing, the Father's love, prophetic ministry, evangelism and more. These deposits are now bursting into flame. I would love to see all this transform the nation, but for all the glory, I think it will stop short of affecting widespread societal changes as I will shortly explain.

Second, the most significant reason we will not see a sweeping culture-changing revival in North America is that our culture and our nation(s) have made a firm decision concerning morality and the role of God in our society that cannot or will not now be reversed. I realize that many may object to this statement, but my reasons for making it bear serious consideration.

In early 2006 I began to sense something prophetically that held a familiar flavor for me, but I had trouble putting my finger on it until I remembered a very difficult sequence of events from my personal life in the 1980s. At that time I ministered in a historic mainline denomination that had once been doctrinally sound, but that had become very liberal theologically—apostate, in fact—over the last hundred years. I became part of the charismatic renewal within that affiliation and served on the national board of directors for the organization that sprang up within it to work for renewal. We fought for a return to a truly biblical foundation and for freedom for the Holy Spirit to move, as we longed to see that venerable old institution restored.

There came a point in 1988, however, when I knew prophetically that the fight for the soul of the denomination had ended. A firm and settled decision had been made against renewal and against both the Holy Spirit and sound doctrine. The course had been set and it would not be changed. Although the arguments would continue, the debate had closed and it was time to leave.

The sense that came to me in 2006 was the same, but this time I knew it applied to my nation and my culture. Despite the prayers of the faithful, we have written God out of public life and in many cases passed it into law. Culturally, we have abandoned the standard of biblical morality and authority, even in the churches. Over time, a societal decision has been made that will not be unmade. Argument may continue, but the debate has ended.

As this decision has settled, an escalating cascade of moral failure and scandal has rocked the North American Church, and I suspect it will begin to affect other Western nations as well, if it has not already. Because these decisions have been firmly made, revival of a massive, culture-changing nature will not—cannot—come.

Every past revival in Christian history has been based on a foundational cultural agreement concerning right and wrong, sin and morality. When society departed from that foundation, everyone knew it. As a result, people could respond to great preaching, feel guilt over their sin, turn to God and repent. Revival grew and spread on the basis of repentance and the forgiveness that flows from the cross and the blood, in large part because everyone understood the baseline from which they had departed and to which they could return. No such cultural agreement now exists. Even in much of the contemporary Church we have lost the sense of sin and, with it, any sense of need to repent. Without a sense of sin, repentance cannot come, and without repentance revival in the fullest sense cannot happen.

So much for the bad news. Now for the good news! God never leaves His people without recourse. A season of the emergence of lighthouse churches and ministries is now upon us. I call them islands of glory in a sea of mud, cities of refuge, places for people to come and find the presence of God, healing and restoration as the way of the world ultimately fails. Places like Bethel Church in Redding, California, or the Toronto Airport Christian Fellowship stand as forerunners of the churches and ministries where those piles of fuel, so carefully deposited over the years, are now bursting into flame. May these and other lighthouses burn long and brightly! Many more are now springing to life in geographically strategic places as God calls them forth.

In short, the world must grow darker as the Holy Spirit burns brighter in the Church. As world systems descend into darkness, the glory of God increases in His Church to draw a great harvest. And then Jesus returns!

16

Four Basic Characteristics of Lighthouse Churches

Presence-Based

A lighthouse church is Presence-based, not dependent upon the show, the slick presentation or any particular formula or program. Focused on seeking and experiencing the presence of God, worship in a lighthouse church is no "in and out in an hour" affair, but lasts as long as it takes to open people up to the real presence of God. Both leadership and laity value the pursuit of the Presence for the honor of the Lord and will not stop until a genuine encounter with God has been achieved.

Freedom for God to Move

God is free to move in any way He chooses. Leadership gets out of the way and allows out-of-the-box things to happen that have not been planned for. Historically speaking, unusual, messy, out-of-the-box manifestations and occurrences have punctuated every visitation of the Spirit that has ever impacted this culture. Wise leaders of lighthouse churches therefore show themselves willing to absorb a degree of messiness. History amply demonstrates that when controlling leadership or a religious spirit suppress manifestations, both the number of salvations and the incidence of miracles diminish. This culture needs and hungers for miracles and the tangible evidence of power. In days to come, words alone will not do.

A Culture of Honor

In a lighthouse church both leadership and laity cultivate a culture of honor. *Honor* by definition ascribes worth, value and significance to people. Lighthouse churches do this for every individual without exception, no matter who they might be, where they come from or what their condition. From top leadership to the lowest of the laity, respect, encouragement and uplift prevail. This can only work within the context of community, a commitment to one another in honor. Light-

17

house churches work hard at relationships and at ministry structures and strategies that foster relationships, knowing that relational love stands at the heart of the Kingdom of God.

A Healing Atmosphere

Lighthouse churches cultivate a healing atmosphere and diligently pursue specific healing ministries both for the physical body and for life's hurts in order to demonstrate the love of God and His restorative power to a world in need.

Refocus for Intimacy with God

It would seem that in days to come we must stop seeking the signs, wonders and prophecies. Such a quest puts the focus in the wrong place. Becoming a lighthouse church cannot be about hungering after power as I see so many of my fellow revival seekers doing. As the events of recent years amply demonstrate, the mere presence of power does not necessarily lead to the creation of an atmosphere of love and safety that both the saints and the world can rely upon.

The goal of our pursuit for these crucial days must be intimacy with God, oneness with His heart. We must plumb the depths of Paul's affirmation when he wrote,

> I have been crucified with Christ; and it is no longer I who live, but Christ lives in me; and the life which I now live in the flesh I live by faith in the Son of God, who loved me and gave Himself up for me.
>
> Galatians 2:20

Power is a by-product of that affirmation. Signs and wonders result from it. This single affirmation forms the basis for all we aspire to become and all we aspire to do.

Conclusion

Let the lighthouse churches arise. Let them gather in the refugees out of a philosophical system that cannot work, that can only wound its adherents, because it disregards and violates the principles on which God built this universe. A lighthouse church is a prophetic church—a prophetic people—because of the impact it makes upon the society around it and upon the individuals who avail themselves of its ministries. "So will My word be which goes forth from My mouth; it will not return to Me empty, without accomplishing what I desire, and without succeeding in the matter for which I sent it" (Isaiah 55:11). Let the prophetic impact be made!

The topics covered in this book represent elements I regard as key to becoming such a prophetic people. Lighthouse churches must incorporate these things and cultivate them diligently. I labor under no delusion that I have exhaustively covered the subject. I can only hope that I have pointed in the right direction.

2

Building a Prophetic Community

Clearly, God has been calling many of us who love the moving of the Spirit to a higher place, a promotion in the Kingdom of God in which we can be entrusted with greater power and authority for victory in life and for cultural penetration. A major component of that higher calling might best be called "prophetic community."

Trust me, a church filled with hundreds of prophetic "wan-nabes" would be every pastor's nightmare. It must therefore be made clear at the outset that only a few members of any prophetic congregation will actually be prophetic persons. God endows the Body of Christ with many gifts, and we need a balance of them all. A prophetic community must first be a community indeed, a people blessed with a variety of gifts and who have been bound heart and soul to one another under God. Second, a prophetic community is a body of believers collectively making a prophetic impact on the community around it. By its very existence, by its love and by the way it functions—all of its parts together—it catalyzes change.

By the definition of prophetic ministry expressed in Jeremiah 1:10, a prophetic community would pluck up things that were never God or that had outlived their usefulness, and it would plant the things of God, releasing power to accomplish His purposes. It would tear down that which opposes the purposes of God or that does not flow from His nature, and it would build up and release the true purposes of God. It would change the course of the lives of individual people and impact the culture around it.

Covenant Community

Currently much of the charismatic renewal wing of the Church has been captivated by an emphasis on power, prophetic ministry and prophetic voices. I say go for it! I am all for the power of God to be demonstrated in this world. However, I see and hear very little emphasis on the foundation for it all. There seems to be too little emphasis on what must happen at the core of our life together. Covenant community!

Understand that if we fail to conquer the influence of the culture around us that teaches us to live as individuals focused on self, and if we fail to learn to live as one in committed covenant community, then all the power, all the signs and wonders and prophetic words will amount to nothing more than just another flash in the pan—here today, gone tomorrow. Historically, most revivals last perhaps five to six years or less before they begin to fade. Often the missing component has been covenant community that would have formed the foundation to sustain what the Spirit gave.

How do we become a prophetic community? How do we become a people who walk in the power and love of God, increasing in miracles and demonstrations of His power, and how can we sustain that for decades to come? My own congregation experienced a dramatic outpouring of the Spirit in 1996 that has continued to the present day, and yet we feel as if we have only begun to experience what God really has in store. So like many others who live mired in Western culture and thought, we struggle to understand the meaning of the covenant bonds that would both propel us into and sustain us over time in the fullness of what God longs to send.

In my own church, we have held a number of prophetic conferences. We have hosted trainings in prophetic ministry offered by internationally known ministries. We have studied power principles and witnessed signs and wonders. Many of us have run from conference to conference both in our own church and in other locations and have taken it all in. We have so many tools in our box we look like Tim the Tool Man Taylor about to use a chain saw to cut paper. And like Tim in that wonderful sitcom we cry, "*More power!*" But none of that will make any long-term difference without community— deep, passionate, consistent commitment to a fellowship of believers with strong interpersonal bonds.

Four Biblical Emphases

In late 2007 the Lord led me to reexamine Acts 2 and some related passages I have studied deeply all my life, and He indicated that I have been missing something in them all these years. If I were really seeing what He wanted me to see, and if the Body of Christ was really getting it, it seems we would be much further down the road to glory and influence as a prophetic community than we are. So I looked, and I saw.

Acts 2:42–45 says that in the days immediately following Pentecost,

> They were continually devoting themselves to the apostles' teaching and to fellowship, to the breaking of bread and to prayer. Everyone kept feeling a sense of awe; and many wonders and signs were taking place through the apostles. And all those who had believed were together and had all things

in common; and they began selling their property and possessions and were sharing them with all, as anyone might have need.

The first thing that struck me in this reexamination was the words "continually devoting" followed by the list of things to which the early Church gave its devotion. The apostles' teaching occupies first place on the list. In other words they devoted themselves to hearing and absorbing what would later become the New Testament. Then comes fellowship, breaking of bread and prayer. Only one item on this list of four evokes an image of a large group of people facing forward as an audience absorbing information. The other three imply, and even require, consistent, deep, passionate covenant relationship between people inspired and filled by the Holy Spirit.

Fellowship means spending time together with other believers in a connected and vulnerable way, sharing lives and being accountable to people with whom you have chosen to share life. Even the most cursory reading of the book of Acts reveals that the people of the early Church spent no small amount of time just being together.

Breaking of bread implies more than merely eating together. In the culture of Bible times, sharing a meal meant much more than our own casual invitation to "do lunch" together, for instance. For people in Bible times, sharing a meal constituted one of the most intimate forms of fellowship possible. You ate together only with people to whom you felt willing to commit in a covenant way. This, by the way, was the element that so offended the Pharisees as they saw Jesus eating with tax-gatherers and sinners. In their view a righteous man would never enter into a covenant relationship with such unclean people.

Finally, *prayer* seemed most often to be something they did together as a unified body. For example, the period of time leading up to the outpouring of the Holy Spirit on the day of

Pentecost began with the apostles and a few others praying together in the Upper Room and ended with 120 pouring out their hearts to God as a body. Hearts bonded as they cried out to God in one accord so that in the opening verse of Acts 2 it could be said that "they were all together in one place," a picture of unity. In Acts 12 Peter had been cast into prison, but the Church prayed as a body for his release and an angel of the Lord led him out. God released power, but it flowed from covenant community!

Continually means that they did these things consistently, while *devoting* means there was a strong focus on these things that deeply consumed them. They chose not to scatter their energy and investment of time into all kinds of other concerns and commitments.

The Source of Awe

Just as soon as the Holy Spirit fell on that original one hundred and twenty a deep, passionate and strong sense of community resulted. Scripture says they "kept feeling a sense of awe." From our 21st-century point of view we might think that their sense of awe resulted from the signs and wonders they witnessed. But note the order of the words in Acts 2:43: "Everyone kept feeling a sense of awe; and many wonders and signs were taking place through the apostles." A sense of awe fell upon them not because of the signs and wonders, but because of the depth and power of the love and fellowship they experienced.

Awe came *before* wonders and signs. The wonders and signs did *not* produce the awe. The passage mentions wonders and signs only once, while the remainder of the passage focuses on all the things they did together in love, and on the sacrifices they made for one another as they lived out their faith in covenant relationship, consistently and deeply pursued.

25

God's Character Imprinted

When the Holy Spirit comes, therefore, He is not first concerned with power. He primarily longs to imprint His own nature and character into us. The apostle John wrote of God's nature: "For God so loved the world, that He gave His only begotten Son, that whoever believes in Him shall not perish, but have eternal life" (John 3:16). Did He do this just so we could live forever in heaven? Hardly. He did this so that we would be delivered from sin and be transformed to look like, think like and feel like Him. The whole of His nature longs to be bound in covenant relationship to us and to bind us to one another in that same covenant.

Jesus prayed it in John 17:21–23:

> That they may all be one; even as You, Father, are in Me and I in You, that they also may be in Us, so that the world may believe that You sent Me. The glory which You have given Me I have given to them, that they may be one, just as We are one; I in them and You in Me, that they may be perfected in unity, so that the world may know that You sent Me, and loved them, even as You have loved Me.

Witness this covenant unity and its effect as the Day of Pentecost unfolded and in the weeks and months that followed.

God calls us to oneness in relationship powered by the heart and Spirit of Jesus. Oneness with God leads directly to oneness with each other. The effect is prophetic, producing fruit that transcends both us and our needs and limitations as human beings, "that the world may believe." This requires a focused covenant community.

Spiritual Polygamy

What if I, the husband of my wife of 35 years, lived half of the time at another woman's home? What if I said to her,

"Honey, I love you. You *are* my wife and this is my home but I just need to live part-time at Mary's house because she has something I need right now"? How stable and effective would our household be? How would that impact our children?

Or what if I informed her, "Beth, honey, you'll always be my first wife, but I just feel I need to be married to this other one, too?" Jokingly I have often reminded her that my Osage Indian ancestors had multiple wives. In response she tells me she is Cherokee and how long would I like to live?

Spiritual polygamy does not build the Kingdom of God. It only keeps us fragmented, ineffective and unproductive at making a prophetic impact on this world. My meaning? The majority of modern Christians attend and even commit themselves to more than one church in a year. I read somewhere years ago that the average number of churches such Christians attend is six. This can never build stable and effective covenant community any more than the kind of living arrangements I described above could create or sustain a stable home. The kind of church life many Christians practice might be more aptly described as spiritual promiscuity, hopping from church bed to church bed seeking the next thrill or perhaps to have personal needs met without real concern for selfless sacrifice, depth of relationships or effective ministry for the sake of others. Interpersonal trust, so necessary to life-changing ministry over time, can only be built in the context of consistency.

God calls us to focused commitment that builds strong relationships in love. The sense of awe the early Church experienced flowed not from the signs and the wonders but from the love they practiced, the connection, the continual devotion to things that made for *relationship* in the power of the Holy Spirit. Prophetic community cannot develop without this kind of "continually devoting."

27

The Apostles' Vision

Romans 12

The apostle Paul understood and taught the value, power and practice of community. "Therefore I urge you, brethren, by the mercies of God, to present your bodies a living and holy sacrifice, acceptable to God, which is your spiritual service of worship" (Romans 12:1). No longer can the Christian walk be built around "me," feeding "me," empowering "me," entertaining "me." "I" must become the sacrifice given up to God for His use and His purposes.

"And do not be conformed to this world, but be transformed by the renewing of your mind, so that you may prove what the will of God is, that which is good and acceptable and perfect" (verse 2). This world practices a way of thinking embedded in the culture that revolves around self and militates against a true understanding of covenant, but God has another way. We must absorb God's mind—which begins and ends in covenant—until our thought life and internal inclinations parallel His. When that happens, we have been made ready to go out into the world and prove God right.

The verses that follow describe His will, the heart of His mindset to which we must be conformed. Verse 3 reads, "For through the grace given to me I say to everyone among you not to think more highly of himself than he ought to think; but to think so as to have sound judgment, as God has allotted to each a measure of faith." Transformation of the mind and heart begins with humility, an accurate assessment of who you are and who you are not. Arrogance violates relationships by taking honor away from others in order to inflate self.

With humility in place, Paul shifts the emphasis to relationship in verses 4 and 5: "For just as we have many members in one body and all the members do not have the same function, so we, who are many, are one body in Christ, and individually members one of another." Connection. Relationship. Covenant. To understand this passage fully we must understand the intensity of the phrase "members of one another."

What would happen if my hand said, "I think I'll go be Mike's hand for a while"? Obviously that would not be possible. The hand would die and I would be crippled. In just the same way, God connects us to one another in one body, not several bodies. He calls us to one congregation, not multiple ones. Unless we remain consistently connected to one another in covenant relationship, the Body of Christ simply cannot function properly. We are neutralized. Powerless.

The apostle continues. "Since we have gifts that differ according to the grace given to us, each of us is to exercise them accordingly: if prophecy, according to the proportion of his faith" (verse 6). In relationship we function as one, although we are not the same. Our gifts differ, like hand differs from foot, as the following verses make clear: "If service, in his serving; or he who teaches, in his teaching; or he who exhorts, in his exhortation; he who gives, with liberality; he who leads, with diligence; he who shows mercy, with cheerfulness. Let love be without hypocrisy" (verses 7–9).

These gifts are not about you as an individual. God does not give them to make you significant or to inflate you. Neither are they primarily about power. They have one purpose only: to bless and love those with whom you have been called to walk. The gifts of the Spirit have no real purpose outside of either covenant relationship with one another or an evangelistic setting in which you minister to someone who does not yet believe in order to bring them into the covenant. Every item on this list implies and demands covenant relationship that already exists or covenant relationship soon to be.

"Abhor what is evil; cling to what is good. Be devoted to one another in brotherly love; give preference to one another in honor" (verses 9 and 10). *Devoted* appears yet again, implying consistency in covenant. For instance, how would you know whether I am devoted to you? You would know because I would be there for you when I felt like it and I would be there for you when I did not. When you called me I would return your calls. I would listen when you needed me to listen. I would be consistent about these things because if I failed to be consistent, then you would see me as undependable and our relationship would suffer.

As the verse indicates, one of the foundational pillars of a covenant community is that we give honor to one another. As you become a part of a covenant community, your whole heart focuses on seeing your brother or sister succeed and advance into the things to which God has called him or her.

Much of the current staff of the church I pastor started out not as finished products but as rather messy people who needed a lot of fixing and development. We took them in and grew them. I am not certain we consciously chose to do this. It was simply the way God chose to direct us. These people have grown over the years until destinies have unfolded that affect the lives of untold numbers of people. This kind of thing forms the heart of giving preference to one another in honor and can only happen in the context of committed covenant relationship.

Honor advances others and gives them room to grow. Honor comes by grace, not by performance. In my own local church I want that dynamic to work for every person who comes to us and for that DNA to be passed on to every succeeding generation of those who join our fellowship. This is a large part of what defines a covenant people, a prophetic community.

In verse 11 Paul adds the intensifier, "not lagging behind in diligence, fervent in spirit, serving the Lord." In a prophetic community we must be passionately devoted to one another. This implies that we know and love one another and that we sacrifice to spend time together. We serve the Lord as one, gathered around a purpose larger than any of our individual parts.

So we continue the apostle's sentence in verse 12: "rejoicing in hope, persevering in tribulation, devoted to prayer." We must be close enough to one another to know one another's hopes and to stand by one another when tribulation strikes. Further, no bond will ever be so tight or the knowing so deep as between those who pray together on a consistent basis or who have labored together at some great task bigger than themselves.

Paul makes it still more practical in verse 13: "contributing to the needs of the saints, practicing hospitality." Covenant commitment must be sacrificial. We spend time in one another's homes. We help materially when anyone has a need. The prophetic impact of this on the culture around us will be that the world believes. The Romans once said, "See how the Christians love one another," as believers conquered the empire with blessing.

"Bless those who persecute you; bless and do not curse. Rejoice with those who rejoice, and weep with those who weep" (verses 14 and 15). Every believer needs to be invested in a circle of people—a smaller group within the larger church— with whom he or she can rejoice and weep because hearts and destinies have been bound together in covenant. In order to do these things with any real depth, we must know one another well.

In context, would it not be fair to assume that "those who persecute you" applies not to outsiders but to those who walk beside you? After 31 years in ministry I know all too well that fellow believers are the ones most capable of persecuting me.

> For it is not an enemy who reproaches me, then I could bear it; nor is it one who hates me who has exalted himself against me, then I could hide myself from him. But it is you, a man my equal, my companion and my familiar friend; we who had sweet fellowship together walked in the house of God in the throng.
>
> Psalm 55:12–14

The proper covenant response to this kind of thing is to bless. Blessing releases and imparts power to overcome offense.

As if to seal up and reinforce his point, the apostle writes, "Be of the same mind toward one another; do not be haughty in mind, but associate with the lowly. Do not be wise in your own estimation" (Romans 12:16).

Hebrews 13

Hebrews 13 opens with, "Let love of the brethren continue" (verse 1). *Love* is a covenant word. Covenant describes a bond and a commitment. You can give love momentarily to a chance stranger. Wonderful! "Do not neglect to show hospitality to strangers, for by this some have entertained angels without knowing it" (verse 2). But this involves little risk and no commitment. Again and again the apostles spoke of the devoted kind of love that develops over time and requires a consistent investment in one another's lives. This is where the contemporary Church in the Western world so often misses the mark.

Verse 3 continues, "Remember the prisoners, as though in prison with them, and those who are ill-treated, since you yourselves also are in the body." In covenant relationship your life is mine and mine is yours. This describes covenant bond. At any given time, my local congregation contains a number of former prisoners. We always have several families with us whose children are currently incarcerated. "Sometime love," a Sunday pat on the back and "Good to see you!" will not meet their need. Hit-and-run compassion misses the mark. They need consistent covenant bonds on which they can rely.

"Do not be carried away by varied and strange teachings; for it is good for the heart to be strengthened by grace, not by foods, through which *those who were so occupied were not benefited*" (verse 9, emphasis mine). *Grace* is the New Testament word for unconditional, unmerited love. *Love* is a covenant word. *Covenant* implies devotion and consistency. Covenant love strengthens us—not the varied and wonderful teachings that saturate the Christian world. These teachings can inspire and equip us, and I love them. I myself deliver them at conferences these days and I write them in books, but these are not the true source of our strength. True strength flows from grace—covenant love.

Conclusion

While I was still in my teens I heard my father share a sermon illustration one Sunday that I never forgot. He told the story of a man who wanted to divorce his wife. The man queried his attorney, "I really want to hurt her when I do it. How can I do that?"

The attorney replied, "Go home and serve her for three months. Bless her in every way you know how, and then, when you serve the papers, she'll be more than devastated." Three months later that man returned to the attorney's office to follow up on his first visit.

The attorney raised his eyebrows, took his pen in hand and asked, "Are you ready to do it?" The man's answer? "Heck no! I love that woman!"

Jesus once told His disciples, "Where your treasure is, there your heart will be also" (Matthew 6:21). Where your relational investment lies, that is where your love will lodge.

Covenant love makes us a prophetic people, a people with something to say, lighthouses of God's healing grace, a people who will change our world. In covenant love we will make a difference to tear down and build up, pluck up and plant.

Very few members of the first church in Acts 2 could be said to be prophetic individually, but they functioned as part of a prophetic community. What they did together and how they lived out their bonds of love made a statement to the world that changed things forever.

Without that bonded community meeting in one another's homes and sharing their worldly goods, all the signs and the wonders would have been meaningless. The apostles' teaching would have been just another set of ideas that entertained and fascinated but produced nothing. New believers just baptized into the faith would have had no place to which to come home and be discipled.

If you led someone to the Lord tomorrow, where would you take him or her? Who would raise them up in the Lord? Babies don't grow and learn to be human by being left in a crib six days a week, only to be held on Sundays. We love babies to life and teach them to be human by holding them in our arms and speaking to them as part of the covenant community we call a family.

For this reason the church in Acts met house to house, devoted to one another, in addition to the large gatherings in the Temple. *That* is Church! When real devotion to one another develops, a prophetic statement is made.

Never forget the forgiveness issue. Family members offend. As a teenager, one of my brothers badly wrecked the family car. Twice! The whole family paid for his mistake because the money required to repair it came out of everyone else's lifestyle. Somebody could not get new shoes. Others wore clothing beyond its attractive useful life. We did not get to see that movie we had all been waiting for. But he was still my brother, the son of my father and mother, and still a part of our covenant. That kind of bond makes a prophetic statement to a lost world when practiced among believers in the Body of Christ, no matter how we fail one another.

Every prophet in the Bible spoke from a foundation in covenant relationship with God and with His people. The bond God institutes, when you move from living as a single individual whom He called to Himself into becoming a functioning part of a people He summoned to model and live His love for one another, looses power and changes cultures. *Love one another as I have loved you.*

If you have been gifted as one of those few who are truly prophetic, then without a solid foundation in a covenant with God that bonds you to one specific local expression of the Body of Christ, you will fail to make whole and accurate prophetic statements.

Trying to be committed in covenant to more than one body at once is like practicing polygamy. You end up being truly close to no one and hindered in your effectiveness to anyone. I have been called as a pastor to build an effective and world-changing community of love with a prophetic impact on a city and a nation, but I cannot do that if my flock is scattered all over the landscape in their commitments. We live in a day when we must practice covenant focus in order to build.

Jesus included this in His definition of the implications of the new covenant that He bought and paid for in His blood.

> A new commandment I give to you, that you love one another, even as I have loved you, that you also love one another. By this all men will know that you are My disciples, if you have love for one another.
>
> John 13:34–35

The signs and wonders that happened *after* Jesus had ascended into heaven occurred either in the context of the kind of covenant community I am speaking of or in the process of creating a covenant community by winning people to Jesus and planting a new church.

I issue a call and an invitation. Desperate for Jesus and for His Kingdom to be full in our midst, I want to know whether Christians of my generation want to be a prophetic community in the cities where God has deployed them. I want to know if they are willing to pay the price in devotion and focus required to build that community—lighthouses, New Testament style. Do it, and we will reap a historic harvest bathed in the kind of awe the early Church experienced in its love. Do it not, and the godless culture around us will certainly bury us.

3

Oneness

The issue of covenant community begs an examination of the true nature of oneness. Oneness stands at the heart of the nature of God that should be—must be—reflected in our lives and fellowships.

Although I have never been in the military I learned something about it through a story told by Lance Wallnau, a conference speaker I once heard on CD. An ancient military commander in a time of swords and shields leads a band of men against a larger and stronger force. The chariots of the enemy come rushing toward them with whirling blades on their wheels—an overwhelming force equivalent to a modern-day force of tanks descending on an unsupported infantry company. As the approaching chariots loom larger and larger he calls to his men to draw closer and closer. At the last possible moment he cries, "*As one!*" and with a shuddering force of impact his men step together in a semicircle of interlocking shields.

They have employed what the military calls a *force multiplier*. Oneness makes them more powerful than the sum of their individual parts, loosing a strength that enables them to resist a force greater than themselves. A force multiplier can be any element that, when added, dramatically increases the combat effectiveness of a military unit. For instance, one man with a bow and arrow might be overwhelmed by a hundred other men with similar bows and arrows, but one man with a machine gun against that same force will easily prevail. The machine gun constitutes the force multiplier. In another example, a larger force of men infected with a defeatist attitude might be overwhelmed by a smaller force fighting passionately for something they deeply believe in. Superior morale makes the force multiplier.

God has built force multipliers into the Kingdom of God and recorded them in Scripture for us to discover and employ. They work in our personal lives as well as in any ministry we might be connected with, and they function in any community of people having a prophetic impact on a surrounding culture. Obviously, the Holy Spirit Himself is the greatest force multiplier of all, but that comes in a later chapter.

You might think that by oneness I mean unity. Please understand that the word *unity* as we have employed it falls about as far short of the oneness I am discussing in this chapter as a single-engine Cessna compares to a Boeing 747. I must confess that after 31 years of professional ministry I have grown tired of laboring for "unity." Although I have worked for unity in the Body of Christ all of my professional life, I have always been disappointed with the results. The idea of mere unity fails to carry us far enough into the mystery of God. Oneness calls us into a deeper place than the shallow waters of mere unity.

Oneness in the Plural Nature of God

Oneness begins with the nature of God Himself from which derives all that is truly prophetic. Deuteronomy 6:4, the most foundational affirmation in all of Judeo-Christianity, says, "Hear, O Israel! The LORD is our God, the LORD is one!" In Hebrew the proper name of God, *Yahweh*, for which Judaism substitutes *Adonai* when speaking it, and which we translate as "the LORD," is singular in form. The singular form for the word "God" in Hebrew is *El*. But with reference to *Yahweh*, only the plural is used, *Elohim*. This affirmation from Deuteronomy 6:4 clearly represents the one Lord as a plurality internally, expressed in the use of the two names, one singular and the other plural.

It would appear, therefore, that the very strength of God flows from the plurality of His nature that exists forever without negating or diminishing His oneness. Christians worship one God existing eternally in three Persons—an unfathomable mystery. This plurality did not begin with the birth of Jesus. It formed the essence of God's nature long before Mary conceived Him, and it constitutes a force multiplier inherent in the very nature of God Himself.

Oneness in the Plurality of Humankind

Man and Woman

God imprinted this same force multiplier into humankind. He created us in His image, to reflect His nature, to mirror Him in some mysterious way not shared by the other creatures. Written into our essential nature is a smaller version of the mystery of God's own plurality in oneness.

Genesis 1:27 expresses at least one aspect of it: "God created man in His own image, in the image of God He created him; male and female He created them." Male and female together as one reflect the image of God more perfectly than either of them alone. Genesis 2:24 reinforces this truth: "For this reason a man shall leave his father and his mother, and be joined to his wife; and they shall become one flesh."

In the two become one, God designed us for strength, intending the oneness of the man and his wife to reflect and resemble the oneness that exists in the plurality of the one God. *Together* they reflect God's image, something infinitely greater than the sum of their individual parts. That oneness, when seen in marriages among the people of God, makes a statement to a shattered world. Power for change multiplies as male and female oneness reveals the nature of God, "in the image of God He created him; male and female He created them." Apart from one another they remain merely man and merely woman, not much different from the other creatures, but created male and female *as one* they reflect an image— God's—greater than the sum of the two of them. One flesh—a prophetic *force multiplier*.

This is not to say that single people do not reflect the image. I mean only that God built a force multiplier reflective of His own nature into the relationship He intended for man and woman.

My wife, Beth, and I—married since 1972—have become one flesh. As we labor together in a joint ministry our oneness produces fruit greater than the sum of our two parts and feeds the lives of others in their marital relationships. If there were two of me, the two of me together would be weaker in ministry and in life than Beth and me "as one." Together we exude a power that looks like $2 + 2 = 8$, and everyone who knows us experiences the prophetic force of it. Bad math but good theology!

No wonder Satan works so hard to destroy marriages and set men and women at odds. He labors to inflame our sin natures against one another in order to defeat the prophetic force multiplier expressed in our oneness and so limit our ability to minister the presence of God in the world.

First Peter 3:7–9 teaches,

You husbands in the same way, live with your wives in an understanding way, as with someone weaker, since she is a woman; and show her honor as a fellow heir of the grace of life, so that *your prayers will not be hindered*. To sum up, all of you be harmonious, sympathetic, brotherly, kindhearted, and humble in spirit; not returning evil for evil or insult for insult, but giving a blessing instead; for you were called for the very purpose *that you might inherit a blessing."*

emphases mine

According to Peter, when man and woman stand together as one and equal, they enjoy a force multiplier with two outcomes in power magnification:

1. *Your prayers are released* and not hindered. In other words, communication with God grows in power and effectiveness. Heaven hears you, as if God were looking down upon your unity to see His own nature reflected back at Him. This He respects and honors.
2. *You inherit a blessing* that affects your life in time and in eternity, but you must fight for it, decide for it and sacrifice for it. It can be difficult to remain "harmonious, sympathetic, brotherly, kindhearted, and humble in spirit; not returning evil for evil or insult for insult, but giving a blessing instead." These keys to force multiplication therefore become effective for us as we sacrifice ourselves for one another, whether we seek oneness with a mate or with others in the Body of Christ. It constitutes the force multiplier that transforms you—and the Body of Christ with you—into a force that cannot be defeated in life or in ministry. The very existence of it releases prophetic power to alter the culture around you as people witness the relationships you share. I have long since lost count of the comments others have made concerning the impact of my own marriage on the lives of others.

Oneness as a Governing Law

God established oneness as a governing law of the universe. It can therefore work negatively as well as positively, just as the law of gravity works either for the good or for the bad depending on what we choose to do with it. For instance, we can use gravity to drop bombs for destruction or we can employ it for blessing as we ski down a snow-covered slope. In either case the same law operates.

For example, there came a time not long after Adam's fall when humanity united in sin. In accord with the oneness principle, this union resulted in a multiplication of force that would have produced a cosmic disaster had God not moved to prevent it.

United in sin and filled with a sense of the power brought about by their oneness, mankind's arrogance grew until they thought to ascend to heaven by building "a tower whose top will reach into heaven, and let us make for ourselves a name" (Genesis 11:4). In verse 6 the Lord responded, "Behold, they are one people, and they all have the same language. And this is what they began to do, and now *nothing which they purpose to do will be impossible for them*" (emphasis mine). A sinful mankind moving in oneness posed a threat even God could not ignore.

Genesis continues: "Come, let Us go down and there confuse their language, so that they will not understand one another's speech. So the LORD scattered them abroad from there over the face of the whole earth; and they stopped building the city" (verses 7–8). God shattered their oneness, the force multiplier that had been focused on achieving something ungodly and thereby prevented a horrible violation from occurring. While they remained one, a force multiplier operated. "Nothing will be impossible for them."

Ministry and the Power of Life Forever

Psalm 133:1–3 reads,

Behold, how good and how pleasant it is for brothers to dwell together in unity! It is like the precious oil upon the head, coming down upon the beard, even Aaron's beard, coming down upon the edge of his robes. It is like the dew of Hermon coming down upon the mountains of Zion; for there the LORD commanded the blessing—life forever.

Oneness among believers releases anointing and empowering for ministry, which is the symbolism of the anointing oil on Aaron, Israel's first priest.

Many of us in the Body of Christ long to see more healing miracles. We pray for more souls to be saved and more lives to be transformed through our efforts. We long to impact our communities prophetically for God. Where true oneness prevails among the members of a local body of believers, the power for these things flows from heaven without hindrance.

The second effect of the oneness force multiplier in Psalm 133 affects the flow of life in general among us. As God sees the essence of His own nature reflected in us, He then sends His blessing in the form of a quality of life reflective of that experienced in heaven. Love. Healing. Joy. Peace. Oneness is a force multiplier that makes us more than we would be as isolated individuals.

Jesus said in John 10:30, "I and the Father are one." Oneness with the Father constituted the source of both His power and His authority. As that oneness extends to us, captivates us and determines the quality of our life together, then power and authority flow from Him through us, as well.

As with the Tower of Babel, even in the world when I played with a professional rock band in the late 1960s we experienced moments of expanded magic when we resonated as one. As one, the power of what we did grew. As one, we played beyond our individual skills and made music we could never re-create. As one, we were more than the sum of our parts: $2 + 2 = 8$. If this works in the world without the Holy Spirit simply because God designed us that way, how much more would it and will it work in the Body of Christ, powered by the Spirit and directed toward a divine purpose? How much favor would be released?

When the church I serve moves deeper into a sense of oneness, I hear more and more stories of advancement and prosperity in personal lives. A force multiplier is at work. In addition to personal blessing, miracles in ministry and openings to touch and bless people outside of our faith abound: $2 + 2 = 8$. We have a prophetic impact on our community, changing people's lives and even the flavor of our surroundings, uprooting and planting, tearing down and building up just by being who we are.

Pentecost

After Jesus had ascended into heaven and commanded the disciples to wait in Jerusalem for the promised power from heaven, they held a ten-day prayer meeting. I arrive at the ten-day figure by doing some simple math. Jesus accomplished the crucifixion and resurrection at Passover. Pentecost comes fifty days after Passover. Jesus ascended into heaven forty days after the resurrection. The difference between forty days and fifty days is ten days from the time Jesus commanded them to wait in Jerusalem for the gift of power until the day of Pentecost. They spent that time in prayer.

Acts 1:14 says, "These all with one mind were continually devoting themselves to prayer, along with the women, and Mary the mother of Jesus, and with His brothers." Note the language, "with one mind." Oneness multiplies force. Oneness opens the floodgates of heaven. Oneness increases the power and effect of the individuals involved beyond the sum of their parts.

Acts 2:1 goes a step further: "When the day of Pentecost had come, they were all together in one place." Oneness. The sound of a mighty rushing wind filled the house, they were filled with the Holy Spirit and flames danced on their heads. Drunk on the Holy Spirit and speaking in tongues, they ended up on the street miraculously praising God in the native languages of those who had come to Jerusalem for the Jewish feast of Pentecost.

As Peter preached—some would say he prophesied—to the gathered crowd of curious onlookers, the church instantly grew from 120 in the Upper Room to more than three thousand. All of this came about at least in part because a force multiplier had been released in a sense of oneness among the 120 that looked a lot like the image of God imprinted upon His people. In response, God poured out His favor and His power. They were of *one mind*, attuned to one another in heart, desire, purpose, guidance and love—2 + 2 = 8.

Oneness in the Prayer of Jesus

In John 17:11 Jesus prayed, "I am no longer in the world; and yet they themselves are in the world, and I come to You. Holy Father, keep them in Your name, the name which You have given Me, that they may be one even as We are." I confess that I fail to understand the fullness of this oneness. I know of no one anywhere who truly does. "That they may be one even as We are." One God. Not three. Three Persons, but not three Gods. One, yet a plurality. Perfect oneness. No strife. No struggle. Absolute harmony in the Three who are One. Our own resonant oneness must somehow reflect the mystery of the oneness of the Trinity inherent in the very nature of God.

Maybe on an infinitely lesser scale it could be something like when my wife and I lead worship or produce music as just the two of us without the band to back us up. So easy! We move together, feel together and breathe together. The anointing flows without conscious effort and ministers a peace to others that we have not found in any other configuration. We know this because of the feedback we receive when we do it.

Or perhaps it might be a bit like the way we sense one another over distances of thousands of miles. In July 2007, I led a team on a ministry trip to Ukraine. Unfortunately, I had to leave behind an unresolved crisis in our ministry for my wife to deal with. Telephones in Ukraine were difficult to come by and so I knew I would have only a couple of chances to call home and that I would have to choose the times carefully. On a particular day, I "felt" her calling to me in the spirit and knew it was time to call. I found her at home, as I felt she would be, and discovered that I had called at just the right time to receive the good report of the resolution of the crisis.

When I was a child my parents took ballroom dance lessons. I will never forget watching them dance in perfect synergy, flawless fluid motion, sensing one another's movements and flowing together without any kind of hesitation or resistance. Oneness would be something like that.

What if hundreds of people in a congregation could move beyond the mere absence of conflict and grow into the kind of oneness with one another that Jesus enjoys with the Father God? What if we could learn to flow together in life and ministry as my parents did on the dance floor so long ago? What if the oneness of our hearts and voices in worship looked like God Himself standing before us like a choir director moving us all in unison? Anyone who has ever sung in a really good choir knows that when all the voices hit a chord in perfect oneness, overtones result that sound like extra voices. Here is the force multiplier that enables us to create things greater than the sum of our parts! What if our worship could truly be His Spirit singing back to the Father and the Son through our mouths moving in perfect unity from the heart? What kind of power might be released in that kind of force multiplier? What kind of prophetic declaration would it make and what strongholds might be broken in the proclamation?

Jesus' prayer continued in John 17:20–21:

> I do not ask on behalf of these alone, but for those also who believe in Me through their word; that they may all be one; even as You, Father, are in Me and I in You, that they also may be in Us, so that the world may believe that You sent Me.

The quality of oneness inherent in the Trinity and imprinted into us has the following outcome in power multiplication. Seeing and sensing the wonder of that mysterious impossible unity, people in the world come to believe our message. Prophetic impact! Oneness validates the word preached because it reflects the very nature of God.

The greatest force loose in the world to discredit our claims as Christians is neither atheism nor government opposition nor opposing religions. Give no credit to Satan. Our own divisions at every level of relationship serve to discredit us more effectively than any other influence possibly could. We keep breaking up the key force multiplier by failing to understand the oneness that goes beyond mere absence of conflict.

"The glory which You have given Me I have given to them, that they may be one, just as We are one" (verse 22). Over and over again Jesus prayed for oneness. One in glory. Glory in oneness. He prayed that we would reflect the image of God, "just as We are one," in the way He designed us to do from the start. "I in them and You in Me, that they may be *perfected in unity, so that the world may know that You sent Me*, and loved them, even as You have loved Me" (verse 23, emphasis mine).

Oneness in the Prayer of Agreement

> Again I say to you, that if two of you agree on earth about anything that they may ask, it shall be done for them by My Father who is in heaven. For where two or three have gathered together in My name, I am there in their midst.
>
> Matthew 18:19–20

Hearing this promise, Peter sensed that the issue of agreement goes deeper than simply ganging up on God. As children, my siblings and I often found our father watching the news on the only television we owned. Bored out of our minds we would march boldly before his easy chair and proclaim, "Dad, we took a vote and we think we should watch cartoons!"

Dad always gave the same answer: "When did this become a democracy!?"

"But we took a vote! You have to let us!" Silence. And the news droned on.

Peter knew that this childish brand of agreement could not have been what Jesus meant. Agreement goes deeper than this and so he raised a question that cut to the heart of the matter. Verses 21 and 22 read, "Then Peter came and said to Him, 'Lord, how often shall my brother sin against me and I forgive him? Up to seven times?' Jesus said to him, 'I do not say to you, up to seven times, but up to seventy times seven.'"

Peter's concern had more to do with agreement or oneness than with forgiveness. In response Jesus spoke of that special quality of oneness that becomes a force multiplier with a prophetic effect—the unity that looks like God Himself and that God respects. Forgiveness is simply the price we must pay to get it and keep it. Peter wanted to know how far that went.

On that note, an associate pastor who served under me once took offense at something he believed I had said about him. I knew that I had said nothing and that he was wrong in his accusation. The words he quoted were not even part of my normal vocabulary. At first, he refused to let it go, and as tensions escalated, the two of us argued in a church elders' meeting for what seemed like hours. I found myself wishing that I had actually said what he thought he had heard me say because then I could have apologized with integrity and put an end to it. I felt powerless.

Suddenly, he stood up, crossed the room, took me into an embrace and firmly said, "I don't care what you said. Nothing is more important than our relationship. Let's let it go."

Is it not time we said this kind of thing to one another on a regular basis? Husband to wife? Wife to husband? Church member to church member? People to pastor and pastor to people? And what if we could do it seventy times seven? Things would change in the Body of Christ as oneness grew, and as a result we would begin to change our world. Jesus said that when two or three gather in oneness, "I am there in their midst," and if "I am there in their midst" is not a force multiplier, I cannot imagine what would be.

Thirty-seven years ago Crosby, Stills and Nash (my favorite rock group during the hippie era) sang, "We are one person, we are two alone, we are three together, we are four for each other." And they had no idea they were being prophetic!

Those who accurately perceive the voice of the Lord today hear a call for the Body of Christ to rise to a higher level in the Lord. Oneness constitutes a major element of the nature of that higher level. We do not yet understand it. I cannot say that I do, at least not fully. But I can sense it and smell it, and I know it when I see it. Oneness, the prophetic force multiplier for a whole people! And together we will win a world.

PART **II**

IDENTITY

4

Rich Man, Poor Man, Pauper or Prince?

I cannot imagine how we could resonate godly oneness with one another and walk in community without understanding who we are in Him. This chapter addresses our status as royalty, as sons and daughters of the King who calls us to walk in the fullness of our identity as His children.

To review: A force multiplier can be any element that, when added, dramatically increases the combat effectiveness of a military force. Illustration: A man in a single chariot facing forty other chariots might have a life expectancy measured in seconds, but place that same man in a modern tank and the fight will be over before it starts. The tank constitutes the force multiplier. God has given His children a fleet of tanks and has revealed them in His eternal Word. When we know who we are in Him, power multiplies.

The Function of Names

Historically, both in the Bible and in tribal cultures in general, names have meaning and serve as a key to defining individual identity. In my own Native American, Osage Nation background, names were and are bestowed on the basis of deeds reflective of one's nature. For example, one of our great chiefs bore the name "Pah-hue-ska" meaning "white hair." He earned this moniker as a young man in battle against the American army in 1791. Having wounded an officer, he intended to take his scalp, but when he grasped the man's hair, his powdered white wig came off instead. Thinking this to be great medicine, he wore that wig thereafter as a good-luck charm. More importantly, for the rest of his life, every time he heard his name he would be strengthened in his identity as a brave and powerful warrior based on that deed in battle.

Abraham

In the Bible the name "Abram" means "exalted father." This must have impacted Abram like some kind of bad joke because he had no son and both his and Sarah's advanced age made fathering one impossible. But God gave him a new name, "Abraham," which means "father of a multitude."

> Now when Abram was ninety-nine years old, the LORD appeared to Abram and said to him, "I am God Almighty; walk before Me, and be blameless. I will establish My covenant between Me and you, and I will multiply you exceedingly." Abram fell on his face, and God talked with him, saying, "As for Me, behold, My covenant is with you, and you will be the father of a multitude of nations. No longer shall your name be called Abram, but your name shall be Abraham; for I have made you the father of a multitude of nations. I will make you exceedingly fruitful, and I will make nations of you, and kings will come forth from you."
>
> Genesis 17:1–6

God changed his identity by means of the gift of a new name in order to strengthen him, to move him from identifying himself as a man under a curse who expected nothing, to understanding himself as an exalted father of many who would inherit a destiny. Every time he heard his name, this new identity would be affirmed, reinforced and strengthened. God kept His promise. Sarah did, in fact, bear to Abraham the son of promise, Isaac. In turn, Isaac fathered Jacob from whom came the twelve tribes in fulfillment of the promise of a multitude of descendants. But it all began with a new name.

Jacob

Jacob, Abraham's grandson, got his name as the second-born twin who snatched after his brother's heel at birth at a time when the firstborn son inherited the father's authority as well as two-thirds of his father's estate. In Genesis 25:21–26,

> Isaac prayed to the LORD on behalf of his wife, because she was barren; and the LORD answered him and Rebekah his wife conceived. But the children struggled together within her; and she said, "If it is so, why then am I this way?" So she went to inquire of the LORD. The LORD said to her, "Two nations are in your womb; and two peoples will be separated from your body; and one people shall be stronger than the other; and the older shall serve the younger." When her days to be delivered were fulfilled, behold, there were twins in her womb. Now the first came forth red, all over like a hairy garment; and they named him Esau. Afterward his brother came forth with his hand holding on to Esau's heel, so his name was called Jacob; and Isaac was sixty years old when she gave birth to them.

As a pastor who spent some early years in the ministry doing pastoral counseling full-time, I understand the "twin syndrome" that seems apparent in the lives of these two brothers. In the restrictive confines of the womb, two babies can compete for space and nourishment. In some cases this results in a deeply ingrained expectation that life will always be a fight, a competition for space, position and resources.

Jacob means "he who supplants," one who trips up another and takes his place, who deceives in order to obtain place and position—a name and nature consistent with the twin syndrome. Although God decreed that he would be the pre-eminent one, Jacob found himself compelled to manipulate and deceive in order to obtain what had been promised to him before his birth. God would have delivered the promise without Jacob's help, but Jacob's deeply ingrained defective sense of identity prevented him from believing it and led to actions that violated and divided his family.

This negative identity received reinforcement every time he heard his name, making it ever more difficult to believe the prophecy that had been spoken over his life. At a heart level he felt, *I will never get mine; there will never be enough for me unless I manipulate to get it. I must manipulate and fool people in order to prosper.* Here we see the poverty mentality operating in one whom God had destined for favor, wealth and royalty.

Acting out this defective sense of self, Jacob stole his brother's birthright in exchange for a meal, but in a more devastating display of destruction, he cheated Esau out of the blessing of the firstborn by deceiving their father Isaac in pretending to be his brother. Aged Isaac had apparently lost much of his visual and mental acuity and could be easily fooled. Jacob knew that Isaac had sent Esau into the field to kill some game and prepare his favorite stew prior to giving the blessing. While Esau hunted, Jacob killed a lamb, hastily prepared a stew and disguised himself as Esau, successfully deceiving their father and tricking him into pronouncing the blessing of the firstborn over him instead of Esau. Understandably, Esau erupted in rage. In order to escape his brother's wrath, Jacob fled, and the family found itself divided.

Next, beginning in Genesis 28, he met his match in a father-in-law with a stronger "gift" of manipulation than his own. First he agreed to serve seven years for Laban's daughter Rachel, whom he loved. Laban tricked him into taking unattractive Leah instead, which probably speaks of "brain damage" in Jacob, who could not seem to figure out which girl he had just spent the night with until the next morning's dawn shed light on the deception! Having been thus cheated of his prize, he protested to Laban, only to be told he must serve another seven years for Rachel.

As time passed and Jacob's two wives produced children, Laban and Jacob engaged in an ongoing game of mutual manipulation. Laban changed Jacob's wages ten times, while Jacob, who carried the favor of God, seemed always to come out on top no matter what Laban tried. God blessed him. Why? Because even though he believed himself to be a pauper, and acted accordingly, he remained a prince by the word of the Lord as prophesied before his birth.

The tension between Laban and Jacob finally escalated to the point that Jacob took his family and possessions and fled in the only direction he could go—toward his brother's territory. Fearing that Esau might still do him violence, Jacob strategically divided his company into two parts so that if one party suffered attack, the other might survive. He sent a gift to his brother in hope of gaining favor and peace and then waited through the night for word from Esau while he wrestled desperately with an angel of the Lord.

Genesis 32:23–30 tells the story:

> He took them and sent them across the stream. And he sent across whatever he had. Then Jacob was left alone, and a man wrestled with him until daybreak. When he saw that he had not prevailed against him, he touched the socket of his thigh; so the socket of Jacob's thigh was dislocated while he wrestled with him. Then he said, "Let me go, for the dawn is breaking." But he said, "I will not let you go unless you bless me." So he said to him, "What is your name?" And he said, "Jacob." He said, "Your name shall no longer be Jacob, but Israel; for you have striven with God and with men and have prevailed." Then Jacob asked him and said, "Please tell me your name?" But he said, "Why is it that you ask my name?" And he blessed him

there. So Jacob named the place Peniel, for he said, "I have seen God face to face, yet my life has been preserved."

In order to establish Jacob in his true identity as a prince, God had to break down the deceiver and manipulator rooted in the twin syndrome, the spirit of poverty. He spent long years using Laban to accomplish that goal, and then physically wrestled with Jacob through the darkest and most frightening night of his life. When he had been broken, when the old identity had been defeated, God bestowed upon Jacob a new name, and with it a new identity that, in truth, had been his all along. Jacob became Israel, "Prince of God," no longer the manipulator who deceived and offended his brother and others. Some sources translate his name as "Champion of God" or "Upright with God." In any case, from that time forward, every time he heard his name spoken, his new identity as royalty would be reinforced.

Perhaps more significantly, the angel told him that he had been granted this new name because he had struggled with God and men and had prevailed. In other words, "You didn't give up. Your bitter root, your struggle, your self-definition got you into all that trouble but in the face of your suffering you never let go of God." Many of us have wrestled with God over long and miserable years. Do not allow yourself to give up! A new name and a new identity await you—although, like Jacob, you may walk with a limp forever after!

After the shift of identity signified by the new name came reconciliation with his brother, restoration and prosperity. Obstacles that appeared insurmountable melted away as the force multiplier of a new identity took effect. The one who thought of himself as a pauper learned that he was a prince and it transformed both his thinking and his life. Because his understanding of himself had shifted, where manipulation once ruled and insurmountable obstacles prevailed, love now governed. Relationships came together.

Simon Peter

In the New Testament, Simon did not become an apostle until Jesus changed his name and identity to Peter, the Rock. Until that time, at the level of his opinion of himself, he remained just a big, dumb fisherman. The Pharisees made fun of him for being educationally ignorant and because he hailed from Galilee—just a man who worked with his hands and stank like fish, holding no position, importance or status.

But when he came to know who Jesus was and is, a new nature and identity began to take root that propelled him into a destiny.

> He said to them, "But who do you say that I am?" Simon Peter answered, "You are the Christ, the Son of the living God." And Jesus said to him, "Blessed are you, Simon Barjona, because flesh and blood did not reveal this to you, but My Father who is in heaven. I also say to you that you are Peter, and upon this rock I will build My church; and the gates of Hades will not overpower it. I will give you the keys of the kingdom of heaven; and whatever you bind on earth shall have been bound in heaven, and whatever you loose on earth shall have been loosed in heaven."
>
> Matthew 16:15–19

In normal Greek usage "rock" appears in feminine form— *petra*. For Peter, Jesus altered the gender to make it masculine— *petros*. After this, every time he heard his new name called, he would receive reinforcement of his new identity in strength— "*Rock*"—as if to say, "You're foundational, Peter. The Church rests on the foundation of your strength and the revelation you've received." So Peter moved from being a pauper, a poor fisherman, to his position as leader of the early Church, a prince of God in the Kingdom of Jesus winning souls, healing the sick and raising the dead. A force multiplier had been installed in his life that made him bigger than he would have been without it.

The Poverty Identity

I grew up in poverty. My father never could admit that fact until many years later because, in the richness of his life as a pastor, he never *felt* poor. Nevertheless we did live below the poverty line materially, and we children felt it acutely. Countless times in the face of real needs, "We can't afford it" shaped much of my definition of myself and significantly weakened me in later life and ministry. Ultimately, each of our lives will be profoundly shaped by whatever sense of personal identity we hold.

As a result, I lived well into adulthood under the curse of a pattern of poverty that repeated itself over and over again. For example, in 1980 I planted a church in Post Falls, Idaho. By 1986 we were ready to build a building on the property the church owned. God's favor enabled us to obtain a loan for which we should never have qualified. The contractor then finished the building for much less than the projected cost. An obvious stream of miracles! But as a leader I labored under an identity as a poor kid that affected everyone under me. Within months of completing the building, and after all those miracles of provision, we stood $25,000 in arrears on payments. The church never grew past a certain point. I seemed to attract only people who walked in the poverty I felt in my own heart and who limited our growth to a level with which they felt comfortable.

In my personal life, God met my every need and those of my family, but we sank ever more deeply into debt and could not understand why. In the depths of my heart I identified myself as one who would never have enough. This ungodly belief concerning my personal identity weakened me and produced poverty and limitation in every area of my life and ministry.

My identity as a poor kid did not stem from the curse of a name. Names in modern Western culture hold little significance, but a sense of identity nevertheless shapes personal destiny and the ways in which we deal with life. In my own eyes I was a poor kid. "I'm not the one who gets blessed. For me there is never enough." As I grew up, this was reinforced every time I asked for something and my father told me no, even when the thing I requested might be a necessity.

For instance, school required white tennis shoes for gym class. My family could not afford them. Embarrassed and ashamed, I had to explain to the teacher why I came to class without the required footwear. Alone I bore the condemnation that resulted. The culture of the 1950s demanded conformity of dress, appearance and behavior. White socks under blue jeans with the light blue inner side turned up in a cuff comprised the uniform of the day for young men and boys. My parents could not afford to buy white socks to replace the colored ones handed down to me by others free of charge. This brought ridicule and persecution from other children, so day after day I wore the only pair of white socks I owned until they turned black on the bottoms, just to avoid the condemnation. Poverty. Poor kid.

Having been brought up during the Great Depression and completely mystified by my misery over the persecution I suffered for nonconformity, my father thought I had what I needed and demanded that I be happy with it, but I faced the deficit every day until it became an identity. "There will never be enough. That's who I am."

For most of my professional life this became the pattern. It went well beyond problems with paying for a building. Every church I served for 28 of my 32 years in professional ministry experienced constant financial shortfall and refused to grow beyond a certain point.

But then God confronted me as He confronted Jacob the supplanter. He wrestled me to the ground and enlisted good people in counseling to help me get at the roots of my dysfunction and break the old identity. Through it all Father God gave me a new sense of self. I am a prince, the son of a King, and I walk in His love and favor.

With the change of identity came a change in my fortunes. A force multiplier took effect that began to work for me and for all who follow after me. Today the church I serve prospers and has growing international and cross-cultural ministries. It used to be that every publisher who contracted for one of my books soon went into bankruptcy or financial difficulty and could not promote my work. Today I publish with a fine publisher that does justice to what God has given me. Good things have happened in my family, between my siblings and me, as well as between my children and me. I am no longer a poor kid and *neither are you* because you have the same Father I have and He is a King. Royal identity—a key force multiplier!

Lighthouse churches, prophetic congregations, have at their core people who understand their identity in Jesus. Because they understand their own identity, they can successfully lift others into theirs.

Royalty in the Scriptures

Ephesians

Ephesians 1:5–6 teaches, "He predestined us to adoption as sons through Jesus Christ to Himself, according to the kind intention of His will, to the praise of the glory of His grace, which He freely bestowed on us in the Beloved." In the context of Bible times, the son of a king inherited his father's wealth and his father's authority. We have become children of God, royal heirs according to promise. We inherit our father's wealth and our father's authority.

The apostle continues with verses 7–8: "In Him we have redemption through His blood, the forgiveness of our trespasses." We obtain this status of royalty because of the blood of Jesus by which we have been cleansed. The price was high but He paid it in love.

He goes on: "according to the riches of His grace which He lavished on us." Strong word, *lavished*! Grace cost Him everything. Unless it has been paid for, you cannot receive your new identity as a prince or princess—and it has been paid for in Jesus at the cost of His own life in hideous suffering on our behalf.

> In all wisdom and insight He made known to us the mystery of His will, according to His kind intention which He purposed in Him with a view to an administration suitable to the fullness of the times, that is, the summing up of all things in Christ, things in the heavens and things on the earth. In Him also we have obtained an inheritance.
>
> verses 8–11

In the present tense. Our inheritance has been obtained. Now. What the King owns we own. No longer poverty-stricken, we have become princes and princesses,

> Having been predestined according to His purpose who works all things after the counsel of His will, to the end that we who were the first to hope in Christ would be to the praise of His glory. In Him, you also, after listening to the message of truth, the gospel of your salvation—having also believed, you were sealed in Him with the Holy Spirit of promise, who is given as a pledge of our inheritance, with a view to the redemption of God's own possession, to the praise of His glory. For this reason I too, having heard of the faith in the Lord Jesus which exists among you and your love for all the saints, do not cease giving thanks for you, while making mention of you in my prayers; that the God of our Lord Jesus Christ, the Father of glory, may give to you a spirit of wisdom and of revelation in the knowledge of Him.
>
> verses 11–17

If you understand the identity and nature of Jesus, then you begin to understand who you really are. Paul continues,

I pray that the eyes of your heart may be enlightened, so that you will know what is the hope of His calling, what are the riches of the glory of His inheritance in the saints, [and again we are not poverty-stricken, but rather rich kids] and what is the surpassing greatness of His power toward us who believe. These are in accordance with the working of the strength of His might which He brought about in Christ, when He raised Him from the dead and seated Him at His right hand in the heavenly places, far above all rule and authority and power and dominion, and every name that is named, not only in this age but also in the one to come. And He put all things in subjection under His feet, and gave Him as head over all things to the church, which is His body, the fullness of Him who fills all in all.

verses 18–23

Note the connection to what follows. Jesus has been seated at the right hand of the Father above all rule and authority, and this defines our position in union with Him.

Even when we were dead in our transgressions, made us alive together with Christ (by grace you have been saved), and raised us up with Him, and seated us with Him in the heavenly places in Christ Jesus.

Ephesians 2:5–6

In some kind of mystery, we are already there! With Jesus we inherit the Father's wealth and authority because we have been—past tense—seated with Him. We are not poor; we have been made the King's kids.

How does this connect with the concept of the force multiplier? If I am only a poor kid, on my own in life with nothing but human resources at my disposal, then I remain weak and ineffective. But if I understand my identity and position as a prince, I walk in the very power and wealth of my heavenly inheritance from the Father who loves me, and I move from glory

64

to glory and victory to victory. I leave a prophetic footprint on the world around me and I shed light wherever I go.

1 Peter

Blessed be the God and Father of our Lord Jesus Christ, who according to His great mercy has caused us to be born again to a living hope through the resurrection of Jesus Christ from the dead, to obtain an inheritance which is imperishable and un-defiled and will not fade away, reserved in heaven for you.

1 Peter 1:3–4

We get to begin to enjoy it now, but even more has been reserved for us in heaven where it cannot be touched or lost, like the child whose rich father establishes a trust fund to which he cannot gain full access until he is old enough to deal with it responsibly.

Romans

For you have not received a spirit of slavery leading to fear again, but you have received a spirit of adoption as sons by which we cry out, "Abba! Father!" The Spirit Himself testifies with our spirit that we are children of God, and if children, heirs also, heirs of God and fellow heirs with Christ, if indeed we suffer with Him so that we may also be glorified with Him.

Romans 8:15–17

Over and over again the Scriptures speak of our inheritance. What Jesus has, we have. We have been made royalty and we need to start thinking and acting like it. Identity leads to destiny!

Continue with verses 18–19:

For I consider that the sufferings of this present time are not worthy to be compared with the glory that is to be revealed to us. For the anxious longing of the creation waits eagerly for the revealing of the sons of God.

We have been made revealers of the goodness, the nature of God, in our identity as royal sons and daughters.

The Challenge

Do we long to redeem a city? A nation? The world? As the kings in a nation go, so goes the land. We need to write it into our spiritual and emotional DNA that we have been placed as royalty in whatever "lands" we occupy, whether it be home, work or neighborhood.

Unfortunately, in the United States and in many other countries of the world, Christians tend to view themselves as victims of legal systems that seek to prevent expressions of our faith in schools, in other public institutions or even on the streets. This mentality results from failing to regard ourselves as royalty who carry the authority and favor of our Father the King, and it paralyzes us where reaching this world and realizing our destiny are concerned.

In my own church we have been working at changing this mentality. For example, in the spring of 2007 a local high school held a talent show as a fund-raiser. Many of our youth group attend there. Word went out that tryouts would be held, but that nothing religious would be permitted. Meanwhile, our youth had put together a "living video," a choreographed representation by live actors of Carmen's recording of "The Champion." In narrative and in music "The Champion" creatively tells the story of the cosmic battle between Satan and Jesus that resulted in Jesus' crucifixion and resurrection, God's ultimate victory over the powers of darkness. Our youth have presented this living video many times in many settings and it never fails to bring audiences to their feet.

The group decided to ignore the ban on religious presentations and boldly tried out for the talent show anyway. Based on our identity as the true authority in this land, as princes and princesses of the King, prayer went up to God. As a result, such power flowed that the teacher in charge of tryouts nearly fell out of his chair declaring emphatically, "You're in!"

At the talent show the student audience behaved rudely for every act that took the stage, mocking and making noise. At first, they did the same to our group, making fun of their angelic and demonic costumes and face paint, but for royalty, opposition can never be the end of the story. Two minutes into the presentation silence fell upon the auditorium, and when it concluded, the cheers and applause were deafening. Youth lined up to ask what church our group came from. They made a prophetic impact in a hostile environment!

We are neither powerless nor poor. We are royalty who inherit our Father's wealth, power and authority. As we understand our identity and walk in it, a force multiplier takes effect and we become more than the sum of our parts, more than merely human, infused with the power of heaven and able to do exploits that would have been impossible to us in our natural state.

Jesus was not a victim of the cross. He *accomplished* it. Paul was not a victim of the beatings he endured or of the prisons in which they placed him. In fact, he ruled in the midst of prison by sharing the Gospel with his captors so that the whole Praetorian Guard of the Roman army heard the testimony of Jesus (see Philippians 1:13).

Polycarp, who lived from 69–155 A.D., could not be made a victim of the flames of his martyrdom. The Romans had to stab him to death to shut him up because he refused to stop preaching even from the midst of the flames. Testimony from those who witnessed the event says that the fire refused to touch him and that his skin glowed like gold. They reported that a sweet odor like incense emanated from the flames. Polycarp understood his status and identity as royalty, and as a consequence, even his death had a prophetic impact on those who witnessed it. Royal identity forms a force multiplier that manifests the power of God to a world hungry to see the demonstration of it.

James 2:5: "Listen, my beloved brethren: did not God choose the poor of this world to be rich in faith and heirs of the kingdom which He promised to those who love Him?" Romans 5:17: "For if by the transgression of the one, death reigned through the one, much more those who receive the abundance of grace and of the gift of righteousness will *reign in life* through the One, Jesus Christ" (emphasis mine).

Renewing Our Minds

"And do not be conformed to this world, but be transformed by the renewing of your mind, so that you may prove what the will of God is, that which is good and acceptable and perfect" (Romans 12:2). When I think like a poor man and carry that identity in my heart, then I have entered into disagreement with God concerning His Word that declares who He is and who I am in relation to Him. Worse, because the world sees me as a reflection of Him, I falsely declare to the world that the Lord Himself is poor and weak.

When I begin to think differently, in the renewal of my mind, breaking my agreement with the lie, then like a prince who has inherited his Father's wealth and authority, I prove the nature of the Lord and His will to bless His children. That will is "good and acceptable and perfect." In other words, my life demonstrates that God's will is good for all concerned, that I stand ready to accept it and that it is without flaw.

We must therefore adjust our thinking about God and about ourselves. Inner healing has become a major and beneficial emphasis in the Body of Christ today and it can help, but only part of this adjustment involves inner healing. We must deliberately and consistently choose to reprogram our minds to think of ourselves as Father God does.

Although we no longer use names in the way people did in Bible times, we can reinforce new and godly identities in one another through mutual exhortation and encouragement. New identities must be established, affirmed and strengthened through repeated reinforcement over time, especially in times of trial, discouragement or disappointment. Part of the call to stimulate one another to love and good deeds (see Hebrews 10:24) involves reminding one another who we are when we seem to have forgotten and when the problems of life have weighed us down.

I can never forget a time in 1991 when discouragement and opposition threatened to rob me of everything I knew about myself. I had accepted a position as executive pastor of a major congregation, not knowing what a mismatch it would be. Every gift I ever believed I had came under attack until I thought I would collapse. Self-doubt threatened to bury me.

At the lowest point, a blessed young woman appeared in the doorway to my office to inform me, "Don't let these people defeat you. You're a thoroughbred. Now run like one!" I remembered my gifts, my anointing and my authority and I got up and ran. Part of it meant leaving that church to plant the church I now pastor, but first I had to remember what God had created me to be.

Learn to walk as royalty and you will activate a force multiplier that enables you to accomplish things bigger than you are, to overcome obstacles that would defeat you if you did not have the authority of our royal Father behind you. Learn to do this together as an army in oneness and we become a prophetic people changing the world around us. We become, in fact, the light of the world.

5

The Light of the World—You

If we must know internally who we are as royalty, then we must also understand who we are externally in our impact upon the world. Jesus said,

> You are the light of the world. A city set on a hill cannot be hidden; nor does anyone light a lamp and put it under a basket, but on the lampstand, and it gives light to all who are in the house. Let your light shine before men in such a way that they may see your good works, and glorify your Father who is in heaven.
>
> Matthew 5:14–16

I sense an urgency for our times surrounding just one line from these verses: "You are the light of the world," with the emphasis on *you*. In contrast to this, in John 8:12 Jesus said, "I am the Light of the world." As believers, we have camped on this statement, and rightly so, because, indeed, He is the light of the world, but in Matthew the emphasis lies elsewhere. In Matthew He told us as disciples that *we* are the light of the world.

In various forms, we Christians religiously repeat certain statements that sound good, but lack a foundation in actual truth. We say, "Don't look at me. Look at Jesus," or, "It wasn't me. It was Jesus." Not bad! We want to be humble, and humble is good, but too often we say these things for the wrong reasons, one of which is that we fail to truly believe what Jesus Himself has declared concerning us. We have not fully understood the implications of the cross and resurrection for our identity as disciples. Too many of us have not really taken on the identity He purchased for us at such a high price. Because of this, we think it holy to attempt to erase ourselves somehow. With all good intentions, we say things like, "I want to be invisible so that Jesus can shine," but Jesus actually taught something more like, "I want *you* to be *very* visible so that I can shine." Never has He wished to erase us. He has rather desired only to exalt us and lift us up before men so the world can admire His handiwork in us. This is the level of His love.

The idea that we must be invisible, that we do not count or that every good thing we do is all Him and only Him is a lie from the mouth of the liar designed to undo what Jesus accomplished for us on the cross and in His resurrection. He filled us with His Spirit, made us whole, forgave us and declared us to be holy. "*You* are the light of the world" (emphasis mine).

Shining in the Darkness

Ancient Near Eastern homes for average people were usually one-room mud-brick structures without windows. With nothing more than a single door to allow outside light into the house, it could remain very dark inside, even in daytime. There might have been a raised area to one side on which the family could sleep, but hard-packed dirt made up the remainder of the floor. A single oil lamp would be placed on a stand where it could light the whole house. Jesus meant for us to understand that the world resembles a house full of darkness containing only one lamp to illuminate it. "You are the light of the world." He meant for us to be seen.

In the first chapter I made a point of emphasizing the accelerating disintegration in the culture around us; if we fail to understand how bad it is out there, then we will fail to understand the importance of the emergence of lighthouse churches made up of many individual flames providing light in a dark place. The world around us is *not* full of light. If our heads remain comfortably buried in the sand and we continue to minimize or deny what is happening to our culture, we will feel little urgency to shine.

Contemporary culture stands on the precipice of collapse as we witness the dissolution of our most foundational societal structures from marriage to the nurture of the young to godly morality. The levels of damage and destruction have risen in recent years until those of us who take our ministries seriously have begun to feel overwhelmed.

In the midst of this, God calls us to be a lighthouse people. Accordingly, Jesus said this in Matthew 5:16: "Let your light shine before men in such a way that they may see your good works, and glorify your Father who is in heaven." We must adjust our thinking about ourselves. Here is the first layer.

Good Works

Jesus urged us to shine so that men might see our good works and glorify our Father in heaven, but I think we often miss the fullness of what He meant by "works." Because so many of us fail to understand our own identity in Jesus as privileged sons and daughters and as royal inheritors of all that our Father in heaven owns, we tend to read "works" as an exhortation to more performance. Work harder! Do more!

"Okay, I'm feeding the poor. I'm manning the food bank. See me? I'm serving in the children's ministry. I'm sweeping the church. I only listen to Christian music. I'm not drinking, drugging or committing adultery. Good works!" The list goes on. And on.

But unbelievers feed the poor. Unbelievers often abstain from the traditional list of sins. We are not unique; the world is not overly impressed by what we do and do not do. The light has little to do with what the world sees us performing. Many of the unsaved perform in the same way! Our "good works" have more to do with the radiance of the Lord's presence flowing out from us to touch the world in ways that cannot be accounted for by any natural explanation.

For instance, the light shines in and through the young woman who came to us five years ago as a methamphetamine addict who had lost her children along with every shred of hope. At this writing she has been clean for five years, her children have been restored to her and she works for a contractor who trusts her to process many thousands of dollars of his money every week. She will be enrolling in university soon to work toward her college degree. The Holy Spirit shines through her! She glows!

Greg came to us as a very lost teenager, experienced the power of God and gave his life to the Lord. For the first three years he attended church regularly, but always came high on something, using drugs to mask the pain he carried from years of childhood wounding. He openly testifies that we simply loved him through it all until his life began to change. Early in 2008 we blessed and commissioned him to serve for two years as a missionary in India.

These things that the world cannot duplicate shed light upon a darkened culture. People see the Spirit of the Lord radiating from lives like that and know that such radiance can only be attributed to something supernatural.

Light shines in the joy and security of the children of a solid and godly home. It radiates from marriages that do not fit the cultural pattern, in which men and women lay their lives down for one another, sacrificing themselves in love to pass a heritage of wholeness and righteousness to the next generation. More than mere human love, there is a supernatural quality to it.

In the 1950s the divorce rate for first marriages in America stood at just 2 percent. Today that rate has risen to 49 percent and, as a result, our children are in deep trouble. We are losing a generation, mostly because the culture has shifted from a foundation in covenant commitment and sacrifice for others to a focus on self that says, "If you don't make me happy I'm taking a hike." This adds up to enormous destruction, unhappiness and burden.

After thirty-five years of marriage to the same wonderful woman, with whom I made three incredible children (now grown and married with families of their own), I often hear people express what an inspiration my marriage and my family have been to them. They say, "How did you do that? You give me hope." This is the lamp in the dark place! These are the good works, not performed legalistically, but simply lived out in the divine wholeness Jesus has given us for all to see.

I have come to know of a number of other marriages and families just like mine. These families shine in the darkness as cultural anomalies. They stand out as those who do not fit. They live by a different pattern and therefore shine in darkness. All we have to do is be who we are. The Spirit of God glows in us.

Let people caught in the darkness of the culture be attracted not so much by what we preach at them, our ideas and our doctrines, as by who and what we are in the Spirit of the Lord. "You are the light of the world."

Becoming a Pastor in Your Place

But you are a chosen race, a royal priesthood, a holy nation, a people for God's own possession, so that you may proclaim the excellencies of Him who has called you out of darkness into His marvelous light.

1 Peter 2:9

Every individual believer has been called as a priest unto the Lord. That makes us all pastors, those who bear responsibility for the spiritual welfare, and even the lives, of those around us. A priest not only ministers to the Lord but connects the people with God, "that you may proclaim the excellencies of Him who has called you." Wherever God has positioned us in this world—as business owners, management personnel, employees, neighbors, families and friends—we stand as pastors to those around us.

I met Pavel on a ministry trip in Ukraine. In the armed forces of the old Soviet Union, Pavel served as a colonel responsible to lead a battalion of men. A young Baptist conscript came into his unit refusing to take the oath of faithfulness to the Soviet Union, regarding it as a compromise of his commitment to God. He had no objections to serving, only to swearing "faithfulness" to anything but his Lord. Not yet a believer himself, Pavel had no idea what to do with him.

As a last resort, he spoke to the man's pastor and they arrived at an equitable solution. The young man could quietly skip the offending word when his unit recited the oath and no one would notice. The problem would thus be overlooked. Nevertheless, Pavel expected that the young man would be a source of disruption and proceeded to treat him as a troublemaker, assigning him all the worst jobs. If a ditch needed digging or a toilet needed cleaning, this young Baptist got the assignment.

After a while Pavel began to notice two things. First, although he had all kinds of problems with all the other men of his unit, this young believer in Jesus humbly submitted to every command without complaint. Second, he began to notice that when the men in the unit experienced problems in their lives, they sought out this young Christian for support and advice. Pavel's perception of and attitude toward this young man began to change. "It was the first drop in the bucket toward the time when I repented and became a Christian."

Because Pavel came to Jesus, his wife came to faith as well. She worked in a support capacity for another battalion where she took a serious risk and began to share Jesus with the political officer, the major assigned to enforce Communist ideology among the troops. Before long, he repented and came to Jesus, but found himself in confusion because his job of promoting Communist doctrine placed him in conflict with his newfound faith.

He sought out his pastor for advice, saying, "What do I do now?" His pastor told him that he must tell his troops about God. The next Sunday the major ordered the entire battalion to church, marching in formation. They filled the back of the hall and listened to the sermon. Afterward, as the pastor issued the altar call, the major ordered these troops to march to the front and receive Jesus. They obeyed.

All this came about because one insignificant believer holding no rank and having no power decided to function as a pastor to those around him. Refusing to turn to bitterness or offense over unfair treatment, he bore a witness that changed the lives of hundreds. His light changed things for ever-widening circles of people.

A co-worker comes to the office looking like the hordes of hell have camped on her doorstep. How difficult is it to be filled with the compassion of the Lord and ask with genuine interest, "How are you feeling? Are you all right?"

Drinking strength and comfort from your expression of compassion, she answers, "I've just been diagnosed with breast cancer. I'm terrified."

You have won access and so you respond, "May I pray for you? Right here? Right now?" She answers with a tearful, "Yes," and you follow through, laying hands on her and expecting a miracle.

All of us encounter people in similar need every day. We need only wake up and pastor them. Jesus performed most of His miracles in the street where everyone could see. As His disciples, should we not do the same? If crossing boundaries in such a bold manner seems too large an obstacle in the beginning, then start by determining to pray quietly in your heart for every person who comes within five feet of you throughout the day and see if the Lord does not begin to break open your heart and provide opportunities to minister freely.

What Hides the Light?

The most significant element obscuring the light for most believers goes deeper than the kind of simple fear or insecurity we all feel when told that we must reach out or become visible as Christians. All of us experience times when we throw up our hands in frustrated ignorance of what to do or how to do it, but even this constitutes a very minor obstacle. Jesus always seems to open doors for those of willing heart. The most difficult barrier to penetrate in most believers arises from our own individual self-definitions. *A self-definition at odds with the one God has for you, the way He sees you, creates a cloud around you in the realm of the spirit that outsiders both see and feel.*

That cloud obscures the light flowing through you from the Holy Spirit who has filled you. People instinctively sense it, and when they discover your faith, rather than see and feel a light that appeals to them, calls to them and lights up their lives, they perceive only that you have a set of ideas—and in this culture ideas are no longer enough. With that cloud around you they regard you as no different from themselves.

Cloud or no, you nevertheless remain the light of the world, a priest to your God and King. If a basket covers a burning lamp, the lamp burns no less brightly. It remains the light just as much as if the basket were removed. Light obscured does not mean light extinguished, but most of us go through life with the basket of a faulty self-definition firmly fastened to our lampstand and limiting our impact upon the world. Yet the lives and eternal destinies of others depend on the light that shines from us. For them our light, or the absence of it, spells life and death.

Most of us learned our faulty identity and self-definition from parents, teachers, siblings and peers. We absorbed the things they said to us, the hurts and wounds they visited upon us, from the things they did and said, as well as the things they failed to do or say. It all comes down to hurtful words, hurtful deeds and love withheld.

The movie *Pay It Forward* tells the story of the small son of a single mother recovering from alcohol addiction. The boy's teacher has fallen in love with the boy's mother and with her son. But then the mother's former abusive alcoholic husband comes home and she allows him in, believing his promises that he has changed. She mistakenly decides to give him one more chance.

The boy's teacher, now angry, confronts the mother concerning her error. He knows what he is talking about because he grew up with an abusive father who doused him with gasoline and set him on fire. As she refuses to listen, he finally explodes, and with desperate passion cries, "He doesn't have to hurt him! All he has to do is not love him!" and the damage is done. Self-definition has been set. Not lovable. Not chosen. Not valued. Ungifted. Unattractive. Unintelligent. Loser. Weak. Poor. How many of us have lived some version of that scenario and have worn that "clothing" all our lives?

By contrast, Jesus taught us to be sons and daughters of our Father in heaven—privileged royalty walking in authority. The Bible resonates with assurances of our royal status, but here follows a sampling and a review from the book of Ephesians:

> Blessed be the God and Father of our Lord Jesus Christ, who has blessed us with every spiritual blessing in the heavenly places in Christ, just as He chose us in Him before the foundation of the world, that we would be holy and blameless before Him. In love He predestined us to adoption as sons through Jesus Christ to Himself.
>
> 1:3–5

Note the use of past tense. Heaven has come to earth in us through the blessing of Jesus, not at some time in the future when we have become good enough or holy enough, and not when we die. Heaven has come to earth here and now, and all because He chose us before the foundation of the earth for this privileged status.

> In Him, you also, after listening to the message of truth, the gospel of your salvation—having also believed, you were sealed in Him with the Holy Spirit of promise, who is given as a pledge of our inheritance.
>
> verses 13–14

The pledge constitutes a real portion of the inheritance reserved for us and guarantees the delivery of the remainder. This pledge we possess now, in real time.

> But God, being rich in mercy, because of His great love with which He loved us, even when we were dead in our transgressions, made us alive together with Christ (by grace you have been saved), and raised us up with Him, and seated us with Him in the heavenly places in Christ Jesus.
>
> 2:4–6

How should we understand the mystery that we have now been seated with Jesus in the heavenly places? Jesus sits at the right hand of the Father in authority. As a present reality we have been seated with Him in that position of royal privilege and authority. What better identity could we adopt?

Adopted as sons and daughters, we have been chosen and transformed. Our Father the King passes to us an inheritance. "You are the light of the world." We need only take the cover off the light.

Personal Testimony

I honor my parents for all they gave me. They pioneered many things in the prophetic movement and in inner healing at a time when to do so drew heavy persecution. Their work set a standard worldwide for the restoration of the Christian family and the healing of broken lives and hearts. As the firstborn, however, in many ways I became the experimental child, the textbook from which they learned as they made mistakes and sorted their cultural conditioning from biblical mandate.

Their culture told them not to compliment a child but only to diligently administer correction. I received this as condemnation and grew up feeling profoundly faulty. I never had the "right" feelings and was told again and again when wounded, "You just shouldn't feel that way." Informed that I was always selfish, I lived under a burden of guilt I could not shake off. Because of the wounding it caused, this only made me more selfish. In addition to all of this, in the world outside the family I felt the persecution my parents endured. All of this meant that I had no safe place to go. I felt faulty, dirty and rejected.

These things eventually coalesced into an identity as one rejected, stolen from, never picked for the team, mocked for being a preacher's kid, poor (and we did live below the poverty line) and never able to reap in proportion to what I sowed and poured out. From inner man to outer behavior I saw myself as the poor kid for whom there would never be abundance. In all of this you see the cloud that would obscure my light for nearly four decades before God began to move in me to remove it.

Absorb this principle: *As long as you allow that cloud to remain, the light radiating from you dims in proportion to your disagreement with God concerning who you are.*

Determine to Renew Your Mind

One of the most useful chapters in the Bible for the purposes of this book is Romans 12, especially verse 2: "Do not be conformed to this world, but be transformed by the renewing of your mind, so that you may prove what the will of God is, that which is good and acceptable and perfect." Consider that this sounds very much like, "You are the light of the world." When my mind conforms to His—first concerning my own identity—I walk freely, unobscured and unhindered, to prove to the world by my life that God is good. Will I live according to what a dark world full of sinners has told me about myself or will I choose to live according to what Jesus has won for me on His cross, in His resurrection and in the gift of His Spirit to dwell in me?

You can go to counseling and get inner healing from now until the turn of the next century and you can get at the roots of your issues endlessly until the day you die, but *until you decide to think of yourself as God thinks of you, to own your inheritance and live like royalty with authority, freedom and a sense of privilege, chosenness and favor, you will remain imprisoned. Decide* is the key and operative word.

God destines every one of us for great things. Why? Because we have a King for a Father. On that basis I have made a personal decision, which I call others to make with me at every opportunity. I will not live the rest of my life at a lesser level of destiny than God has ordained for me. I will not live wrapped in the cloud and so cheat the people I love, as well as the people whom I will come to love, out of the glory that is my birthright to dispense. I challenge others to make the same determination.

I refuse to live the rest of my life under the cloud of lies and, to the extent that it lies within my power, I will not allow my brothers and sisters in the Lord to do it either. On that score I have been filled with righteous wrath to bring my own thinking, my own mind and my own attitude about myself into alignment with the Word of God. With the same intensity of purpose, I will help others to do so as well. I choose to be intolerant of any thought or attitude in me that does not line up with my God-given identity. I will both believe and live what He has given me.

If I have learned anything in more than three decades of ministry, it is that righteous beliefs and attitudes never happen by accident. Moods and feelings cannot spawn them. Lifetime beliefs and attitudes never result from some outside stimulus. These things result from *decisions* made internally with determination and perseverance by hungry and desperate people who have decided to live as God designed them to live in the power of the Holy Spirit.

Ultimately, they make this determination not for their own sake but out of desperation for others in love, and that is what makes it work. Self leads to death while sacrifice leads to life. So it starts with family, then friends and other believers. Finally it extends to the world. Your heart cries, *I want to know that I lived for something, that when I go to heaven I can say, "I did it! I did it all! And it was fun!"*

Conclusion

You *are* the light of the world, but you must take the cover off of the light. Many of us have been wrapped in the darkness of a faulty self-definition all our lives. I speak not only of poor people and troubled ones, but of business owners, managers, nurses, financial planners and others who appear outwardly successful and well-adjusted. At various levels, we all share the same crippling affliction.

Faulty self-definition does *not* have the power to make you less than Jesus declares you to be. No matter what, you remain the light of the world, but your self-definition can cover the light like a basket. For this reason Jesus commands us not to allow it to be covered. You are what you are. You might as well agree with Him.

Having broken agreement with the lies of the enemy of our soul, we enter into agreement with God by seeking out every thought, every feeling and every attitude that fails to line up with what it means to be adopted through the blood of Jesus as a son or daughter of the King of the universe. We must become intolerant of those thoughts, attitudes and feelings and make war on them. Say in your heart, *I am* not *going to live that way.*

Do so, and you will become a cultural anomaly, a glorious misfit standing out in the company of ordinary men and women. The goodness radiating unhindered from you will light up the world around you. People will be touched by something infinitely greater than your ideas and theological propositions. These can leave them cold because they have heard them before. It will rather be the power and love of the living God that impacts them through you.

People will come to the lighthouse that you have become and to the lighthouse your church has become, and there they will see and feel something good and wholesome, so at contrast with the world that they will be mystified by it and will feel compelled to ask about it. They will feed on your health, your relationships, your marriage, your joy, your peace and the stability of your children, and they will be made healthy themselves just by being exposed to it.

Come into agreement with God concerning you. He is right. You are wrong. Give it up.

Finally, feed your inner person on the following passage. Declare it over and over again to yourself and reprogram the computer of your mind with it until the new programming overwrites the old. "He made Him who knew no sin to be sin on our behalf, so that we might become the righteousness of God in Him" (2 Corinthians 5:21). Now condense this to a pair of affirmations. I have found that few have trouble with the first one, but that many have trouble with the second. Work with them both!

1. *We are the light of the world. We are the righteousness of God.*
2. I am the light of the world. I am the righteousness of God. Believe it. Live it. Shine it!

PART **III**

DESTINY

6

The Daniel-Joseph Anointing

As I outlined in the previous chapter, I tell the members of my congregation that each of them is a "pastor in your place." Imagine the light-giving prophetic impact of an army of believers deployed into the world and functioning as the priests they were called to be, according to 1 Peter 2:9. God makes a pastor responsible for the spiritual wellbeing of those under his or her care. Each of us bears responsibility for the spiritual wellbeing of those among whom we have been deployed, whether at home, at work, at school or in the neighborhood. Both Daniel and Joseph serve as models for how this can be done, and at the same time their lives illustrate principles of force multiplication by which to magnify our impact on the world around us.

Four Stages of Anointing in Daniel

The Daniel-Joseph anointing comes in four stages and with certain conditions attached.

In Daniel's day, Babylon, an empire that had never known his God, had destroyed his nation. The people of Israel had been deported to live in exile in Babylon, the region we now know as Iraq. Cut off from his homeland and trapped in a place of foreign language and customs, Daniel could easily have assumed the role of a persecuted minority and acted in weakness and bitterness, but he did not. Instead he chose a path of honor and servanthood that led to a significant prophetic impact on a foreign king and an entire nation.

Stage One: Captivity and/or Persecution

The first stage of the Daniel-Joseph anointing is captivity and/or persecution. For Daniel this began as an assault on his culture and heritage as a Jewish man dedicated to his faith and as pressure to compromise the principles of God. While Daniel was yet a young man, the Babylonian king began a policy of systematic suppression of both his faith and his identity.

> Then the king ordered Ashpenaz, the chief of his officials, to bring in some of the sons of Israel, including some of the royal family and of the nobles, youths in whom was no defect, who were good-looking, showing intelligence in every branch of wisdom, endowed with understanding and discerning knowledge, and who had ability for serving in the king's court; and he ordered him to teach them the literature and language of the Chaldeans.
>
> Daniel 1:3–4

Daniel found himself conscripted into a program in which it became illegal to live as a Jew. But he possessed wisdom, spiritual gifts and essential knowledge of which the king would later desire to avail himself.

As the training began,

> The king appointed for them a daily ration from the king's choice food and from the wine which he drank, and appointed

that they should be educated three years, at the end of which they were to enter the king's personal service. Now among them from the sons of Judah were Daniel, Hananiah, Mishael and Azariah. Then the commander of the officials assigned new names to them; and to Daniel he assigned the name Belteshazzar, to Hananiah Shadrach, to Mishael Meshach and to Azariah Abed-nego.

verses 5–7

The king deprived them even of their names, intending to erase their Jewish identity and to mold them into servants of the governmental system of the empire, which included immersing them in both its philosophy and its religion.

But Daniel made up his mind that he would not defile himself with the king's choice food or with the wine which he drank; so he sought permission from the commander of the officials that he might not defile himself.

verse 8

Jews practiced dietary laws handed down in the Torah, but now the king ordered Daniel and his friends to compromise those laws. The issue was never food, but rather religion and loyalty to the one true God.

Daniel therefore stood his ground, appealed to the commander for an exemption and proved that abiding by the Law of God produces a better result than compromise. The anointing, power and position in which he would later walk depended on how he dealt with persecution. In the years to come he would face similar tests repeatedly.

Stage Two: Servant Heart and Gifting

Stage two of the Daniel-Joseph anointing is development of a servant heart, together with the spiritual gifting to make it effective. The time came when the king had a dream that neither he nor his wisest counselors could interpret.

89

Furious, the king ordered the execution of all his wise men for their failure. Although Daniel had not yet been given opportunity to interpret the dream, he would have been among the slain had he not chosen to assert himself in the king's service.

Daniel 2:13–16 begins the story:

> So the decree went forth that the wise men should be slain; and they looked for Daniel and his friends to kill them. Then Daniel replied with discretion and discernment to Arioch, the captain of the king's bodyguard, who had gone forth to slay the wise men of Babylon; he said to Arioch, the king's commander, "For what reason is the decree from the king so urgent?" Then Arioch informed Daniel about the matter. So Daniel went in and requested of the king that he would give him time, in order that he might declare the interpretation to the king.

Daniel and his friends immediately turned to prayer—not prayer *against* the king, but rather prayer for favor that they would be able to *serve* the king and interpret the dream. When the pressure of persecution comes to bear through whatever authority structure you must live under, never simply surrender. Pray, but not for judgment. Pray for revelation and wisdom that you might demonstrate the power of your God to those who do not yet know Him. In response to their fervent prayers, verse 19 says that God revealed the dream to Daniel in a night vision. As he shared it with the king, he delivered himself and the king's men from death.

Increasingly Christians find themselves thrust into positions in which authorities tell us to suppress our Christian identity and to compromise both our moral commitments and our culture. Authorities ask us to do things that violate the moral code under which we live. This constitutes captivity because each of us must work in order to make a living and because we cannot escape the world in which we live. It is persecution because it threatens economic or other forms of harm for the simple act of living out our identity in the Lord.

In response to this kind of threat, Daniel stood his ground and turned to the wisdom God had given him. He used his prophetic gift of dream interpretation to serve the king and so gained favor.

When he came to the king with the answer to the riddle of the dream, notice that Daniel clearly stated the source of his revelation. Never did he compromise his identity as a believer or surrender his obligation to let others know that the God he served was the source of his wisdom.

> Daniel answered before the king and said, "As for the mystery about which the king has inquired, neither wise men, conjurers, magicians nor diviners are able to declare it to the king. However, there is a God in heaven who reveals mysteries, and He has made known to King Nebuchadnezzar what will take place in the latter days. This was your dream and the visions in your mind while on your bed."
>
> Daniel 2:27–28

Stage Three: Favor and Position

The third stage of the Daniel-Joseph anointing brings favor and position. Daniel 2:46–49 reads,

> Then King Nebuchadnezzar fell on his face and did homage to Daniel, and gave orders to present to him an offering and fragrant incense. The king answered Daniel and said, "Surely your God is a God of gods and a Lord of kings and a revealer of mysteries, since you have been able to reveal this mystery." Then the king promoted Daniel and gave him many great gifts, and he made him ruler over the whole province of Babylon and chief prefect over all the wise men of Babylon. And Daniel made request of the king, and he appointed Shadrach, Meshach and Abed-nego over the administration of the province of Babylon, while Daniel was at the king's court.

Might Revelation
Jim Brog. 1/31/09.

When a persecuted Christian stands his or her ground, becomes a servant in the face of difficulty and uses the gifting of the Holy Spirit to bless an ungodly employer or to aid an unfriendly neighbor, the resulting opposition can feel like captivity. You may be unjustly persecuted just for being who Jesus made you to be, but in the end, favor and position result, provided you refuse to allow yourself to be put off or intimidated by the initial opposition. In seeking God for wisdom to bless and benefit those who appear to be enemies, you will be the one with answers, wisdom and integrity when the chips are down. Wisdom and integrity bring favor and position.

One of our church members worked in a convalescent facility where the corporate atmosphere seemed hostile not only to her faith but to any real sense of team. Not a pleasant working environment! Much prayer went into finding a way for her to bear a witness and move in godly authority in that setting. She began by becoming a humble servant who prayed blessing over the facility.

During this same period of time, my wife introduced a kind of game to our congregation designed to help our people overcome negativity and grumbling. The idea was to go thirty days without complaining. As a reminder, the participant placed a pink plastic bracelet on one wrist. Each time the participant caught himself/herself complaining, the count started again from zero and the bracelet moved to the other wrist.

Our church member took this idea to her workplace and began to distribute wristbands. It caught on until employees began to come, one by one, asking if they could have one, too. Not long after this, she began giving a daily word from Scripture over the facility's intercom system—something that would have been impossible only months prior. This became so cherished by the residents that when she neglected to give it, residents raised a cry of dismay, "Where's the daily word?" Servanthood leads to favor and position and opens the hearts of the ungodly to make room for our God.

But even when favor has been given, persecution may not cease. After Daniel had been exalted to high position in the Babylonian government, his friends Shadrach, Meshach and Abed-nego faced the fiery furnace heated seven times for their refusal to worship the image of the king. A spirit of assassination on the part of other servants of the king worked to precipitate that threat. How many of us have encountered similar situations in the workplace at one time or another? Servanthood and blessing land you a higher position in the company for which you work. This incites jealousy on the part of co-workers, who then insinuate lies and distortions designed to discredit and destroy.

I love the outcome in 3:28–30:

Nebuchadnezzar responded and said, "Blessed be the God of Shadrach, Meshach and Abed-nego, who has sent His angel and delivered His servants who put their trust in Him, violating the king's command, and yielded up their bodies so as not to serve or worship any god except their own God. Therefore I make a decree that any people, nation or tongue that speaks anything offensive against the God of Shadrach, Meshach and Abed-nego shall be torn limb from limb and their houses reduced to a rubbish heap, inasmuch as there is no other god who is able to deliver in this way." Then the king caused Shadrach, Meshach and Abed-nego to prosper in the province of Babylon.

Later on came the incident in the lions' den when Daniel refused the king's decree that required him to stop praying to God and pray only to the king. Again, assassins in the king's hierarchy who felt jealousy toward Daniel deceived the king in order to trap Daniel. They led the king to pass a law that Daniel could not obey, but because his service had won him favor, when the king discovered the ruse and understood that he could not rescind his own law, he fasted and prayed to ensure Daniel's deliverance.

It gets even better. In 6:24,

The king then gave orders, and they brought those men who had maliciously accused Daniel, and they cast them, their children and their wives into the lions' den; and they had not reached the bottom of the den before the lions overpowered them and crushed all their bones.

With favor and position comes vindication.

Stage Four: Release and Exaltation

The final phase is release and exaltation. Following Daniel's deliverance from the lions' den, the king made a proclamation:

> "I make a decree that in all the dominion of my kingdom men are to fear and tremble before the God of Daniel; for He is the living God and enduring forever, and His kingdom is one which will not be destroyed, and His dominion will be forever. He delivers and rescues and performs signs and wonders in heaven and on earth, who has also delivered Daniel from the power of the lions." So this Daniel enjoyed success in the reign of Darius and in the reign of Cyrus the Persian.
>
> Daniel 6:26–28

Daniel won not only his own life but also honor and glory for the God he served. He remained a chief advisor through the reign of three kings—Nebuchadnezzar, Darius and Cyrus.

This is the way of the Christian in a hostile world, even in a world more hostile than ours. This is how believers succeed and advance in life. Test this word and find it to be true! But do not expect to be exempt from persecution. The test may lie in whether you believe that your employer is your provider or that your supply comes from the God of heaven. If you see your employer as your source of provision, then you will remain quiet and behave just like everyone else, but if you know that God sustains your life, you will stand your ground in faith and determine to function as a servant. This test faced Daniel and it confronts us as well. In days to come such tests will only increase in frequency and intensity.

You can choose to compromise and remain insignificant or you can decide to stand and serve even unrighteous authorities with all your wisdom and all your spiritual gifts while letting them know who you are and whom you serve. Choose the latter and you will ultimately see yourself favored, sought after and finally released into higher position. Prophetic impact!

Four Stages of Anointing in the Life of Joseph

Centuries before Daniel, Joseph underwent a similar experience, although Joseph's character seemed much less laudable at first. His brothers, fed up with his arrogance, sold him into slavery in Egypt. Whatever you might think of them for perpetrating such a heinous crime, Joseph clearly brought it on himself. Whether or not he deserved what he got, the outcome put him in the same situation Daniel would later occupy—a believer in captivity about to suffer persecution among those who knew nothing of his God.

A wealthy and influential man named Potiphar became his master.

> Now his master saw that the LORD was with him and how the LORD caused all that he did to prosper in his hand. So Joseph found favor in his sight and became his personal servant; and he made him overseer over his house, and all that he owned he put in his charge. It came about that from the time he made him overseer in his house and over all that he owned, the LORD blessed the Egyptian's house on account of Joseph; thus the LORD's blessing was upon all that he owned, in the house and in the field.
>
> Genesis 39:3–5

As with Daniel, the story began with captivity, but in a dramatic illustration of transformation, Joseph quickly grew into stage two—the servant heart and gifting. Having learned wisdom early in his captivity, Joseph used his gifts to bless the man who owned him and therefore earned a promotion to stage three—favor and position.

Your future, your advancement, your life and wellbeing depend not upon your circumstances. We have been called not as victims, but to rule and reign no matter where we find ourselves. Your advancement and your future are therefore never subject to circumstances but rather to how you respond to circumstances. His brothers forced Joseph into slavery, but he rose to favor and position because of his servant heart as he used his abilities to bless his master.

But remember that persecution may not cease with the gift of favor. Genesis 39:7 tells us, "It came about after these events that his master's wife looked with desire at Joseph, and she said, 'Lie with me.'" After suffering his righteous refusal on more than one occasion, Potiphar's wife vented her spite by accusing him of attempting to violate her. Joseph landed in prison. Back to stage one—captivity and persecution!

Once more Joseph faced the choice of surrendering to the tendency to whine over the injustice done him, or choosing to become a servant. Considering all he had done for the Lord, he might have felt that he certainly did not deserve this! In a similar situation many of us might protest, "I tried it and it didn't work." Joseph chose the servant heart and spiritual gifting in the face of a devastating setback—stage two once more.

In making this choice he ceased to be a victim of unjust treatment and rose to be the supervisor over the jail, even while still imprisoned there. Stage three—favor and position!

In this position of favor, while yet in prison, he met the Pharaoh's cupbearer who had drawn a jail sentence for some kind of offense against the king. This cupbearer had a dream for which he sought an interpretation. Joseph used his prophetic gift to interpret the dream, not in order to gain favor but because he had learned to be a servant and to use what God had given him to serve and bless others.

Upon his release the king's servant resumed his service to Pharaoh. Two years later Pharaoh himself had a dream that no one could interpret, at which point the cupbearer suddenly remembered Joseph and alerted Pharaoh to send for him. Joseph graciously interpreted the dream as a warning from God concerning a coming seven-year famine, and he outlined a plan for dealing with it.

Here is a key. Before he interpreted the dream, Joseph made certain Pharaoh knew who he really was. Any who would walk in the Daniel-Joseph anointing must determine never to compromise their Christian identity or conceal it in any way. "Joseph then answered Pharaoh, saying, 'It is not in me; God will give Pharaoh a favorable answer'" (Genesis 41:16).

This gets him stage three, favor and position, but more than favor and position, he moved into stage four, release and exaltation.

> So Pharaoh said to Joseph, "Since God has informed you of all this, there is no one so discerning and wise as you are. You shall be over my house, and according to your command all my people shall do homage; only in the throne I will be greater than you." Pharaoh said to Joseph, "See, I have set you over all the land of Egypt." Then Pharaoh took off his signet ring from his hand and put it on Joseph's hand, and clothed him in garments of fine linen and put the gold necklace around his neck. He had him ride in his second chariot; and they proclaimed before him, "Bow the knee!" And he set him over all the land of Egypt. Moreover, Pharaoh said to Joseph, "Though I am Pharaoh, yet without your permission no one shall raise his hand or foot in all the land of Egypt."
>
> verses 39–44

A Pastor in Your Place

Do you feel like a captive at your place of work? Is it difficult to be a Christian? Do persecution, hatred, ridicule or even threats of loss come to you? Stand your ground in grace and love. Become a "pastor in your place."

Being a pastor in your place does not mean you have been given a license to preach and make yourself obnoxious; it means you have been given a mandate to serve and to use your spiritual gifts to help, to bless and to give wisdom wherever and whenever you can, and then to quietly and respectfully let people know why and in whose power you do it. This is stage two, the servant heart and spiritual gifting.

My wife, Beth, serves as the children's minister at our church. In that capacity God gave her a vision to impact local grade schools. Beginning with the elementary school that some of our grandchildren attended, she went in as a servant, helping teachers in practical ways to set up bulletin boards and organize events. In a culture in which God has been ruled out of public schools and prayer has been prohibited, she won the trust of the school principal, who then began phoning her with prayer requests for students and faculty. As she prayed, things at the school began to change. As evidence of change mounted, the principal granted permission to pray through the halls of the school at will. Prophetic impact through servanthood!

Daniel blessed the unrighteous king who persecuted him. He served him and did him good, and it brought favor and a higher position. This was stage three—favor and position. Time in prison broke Joseph's heart and made him a humble servant ready to serve an unbelieving and unrighteous king. For that God granted him favor and position.

I can say with certainty that some of us have been thrust into captivity in various situations until, in humility, we learn the servant heart that leads us to use our gifts to bless even the unrighteous. God puts us in such situations because He *wants* to give us favor and position.

Because this lesson is so central to the heart of Jesus, this means that some of us will remain in the difficult situations in which we have been placed until we learn it. Hideously abused and hanging on a cross to pay for sins He did not commit, Jesus served us, and it led directly to stage four, release and exaltation.

> For this reason also, God highly exalted Him, and bestowed on Him the name which is above every name, so that at the name of Jesus every knee will bow, of those who are in heaven and on earth and under the earth, and that every tongue will confess that Jesus Christ is Lord, to the glory of God the Father.
>
> Philippians 2:9–11

Are we disciples of Jesus or merely camp followers? Are we victims or victors who rise above circumstances no matter where we are? Are we part of the world, or are we world changers? Are we ordinary people, or are we priests of the Most High God who exercise His heart, His wisdom and His love no matter what unjust system we might find ourselves laboring under?

We must remember and study Daniel in his position of trust, as well as Joseph presiding over all of Egypt, second only to the king. Above all we must study Jesus on whom the Father has bestowed the name that is above every name that every knee should bow and confess Him as Lord. In this way we will become a prophetic people bringing light and change in every place into which our Father has sent us.

7

Force Multipliers: Moses

In earlier chapters I have written of force multipliers. Time to restate the definition: A force multiplier is a factor that, when added, dramatically increases (hence "multiplies") the combat effectiveness of a military force. Where prophetic impact, or even our lives are concerned, force multipliers make us bigger and stronger than we would be as one man or one woman alone. With force multipliers in play, one person or a small group of people can overcome overwhelming obstacles and make an impact on the world around them.

Moses stands as the most towering figure of the Old Testament. He faced down and defeated Pharaoh, the most powerful monarch in the world at that time. He parted the Red Sea and drew water out of rocks. Ultimately he molded a few hundred thousand contentious slaves into a cohesive nation with a faith, a common identity, a governing legal code and the military potential to conquer a land and drive out a people stronger than they were.

You might think in your heart, *Well, he was Moses. I'm me. He was special. I'm not.* But if that is what you think, then most of the Bible will be nothing more than a storybook to you, having little relevance for you personally.

To comprehend the reality and the relevance, let us begin by doing away with the Charlton Heston image (exuding authority with his rich voice and dignified bearing) and let us see clearly the real Moses, beginning with the part where he became a murderer. He killed an Egyptian taskmaster for beating a Hebrew slave, for which even his own people mocked him, and then he fled Egypt to escape the penalty of death at the hand of Pharaoh.

Despite having been adopted by Pharaoh's daughter, Moses could not therefore have stood in the kind of high favor with Pharaoh that the movies would have us believe. If that had been the case, he would have enjoyed some degree of royal immunity for his actions. Instead, he became an outcast, not knowing who he was or where he truly belonged.

His wanderings led him to the land of Midian, where he found the seven daughters of Jethro, the priest, laboring at the well to draw water for their flock against opposition and harassment from a group of shepherds. Moses fought for them, thus winning the favor of their father, who rewarded him by granting one of his daughters as a wife.

For perhaps forty years or so he lived quietly in Midian herding sheep and making babies. Until the appearance of the burning bush interrupted his tranquility, he remained nothing more than a husband, a father and a keeper of sheep, apparently never dreaming of himself as a leader.

Destiny Intrudes

At this point the great challenge of his life presented itself. From the midst of the flames, which burned but did not consume the bush, God summoned him to go to Egypt and speak to Pharaoh to set His people free. A fascinating dialog unfolds, beginning in Exodus 3:11 when he objected, "Who am I?" meaning, "I'm nobody. Insignificant. Nothing."

Moses continued. "Behold, I am going to the sons of Israel, and I will say to them, 'The God of your fathers has sent me to you.' Now they may say to me, 'What is His name?' What shall I say to them?" (Exodus 3:13). He meant, "I don't know who You are." When God calls you, you might object, "I don't know enough about God. I'm not ready." I hear this objection repeated by all kinds of believers casting about for valid reasons to sidestep the call of God.

Moses persisted! "What if they will not believe me or listen to what I say? For they may say, 'The LORD has not appeared to you'" (Exodus 4:1). In other words, "I have no credibility. I'm going to tell them about a burning bush that didn't burn. Right. And they'll say, 'Did that bush have little pointy leaves and a funny smell? Did you inhale?'"

Finally he raised the issue of his lack of gifting: "Please, Lord, I have never been eloquent, neither recently nor in time past, nor since You have spoken to Your servant; for I am slow of speech and slow of tongue" (Exodus 4:10). In short, Moses protested, "I'm an ungifted nobody with no leadership skills! I can't do this! Get somebody else!" Every day as a pastor I see too many believers walking in, and being weakened by, this same set of ungodly beliefs concerning gifts, abilities, place and position. Moses was no different from you and me and maybe even a bit worse. A few verses later we find him begging desperately to be released from this calling. Not one to be easily dissuaded, he persisted until at last God lost patience and erupted in anger. Fortunately, this served to turn Moses' heart. He obeyed and destiny unfolded.

Moses' Force Multipliers

Obviously this weak, ungifted nobody from the distant and unimportant land of Midian needed some force multipliers in his life in order to perform the most significant and monumental task God had ever assigned to any human being up until that time.

Boldness

Boldness did not come naturally to Moses. Because it seems he was a whiny coward by nature, he had to actively choose it. "Please send somebody else! I don't speak well. I don't have the gifts for it." In order to go before Pharaoh, Moses had to consciously and deliberately choose boldness, not merely wait to feel it. Those who passively wait to feel boldness will probably never experience it.

Once again, take care to delete those mental images of Charlton Heston marching into the throne room of Pharaoh exuding confidence and authority and speaking eloquently with an impossibly rich and commanding voice. In reality Moses went boldly before Pharaoh in spite of his fear, but first he made his brother, Aaron, stand between him and Pharaoh and do all the talking. Scripture tells us that God gave Aaron to Moses as a spokesman to compensate for Moses' deficiencies as a public speaker, but one might wonder how much it had to do with Moses thinking, *If they kill Aaron first, I'll have time to run for the door*. I can imagine Moses internally quaking with fear, fully aware of the possibility of his imminent and painful demise.

However, boldness overcomes fear and therefore becomes a force multiplier. Boldness in obedience to God magnifies power. At Moses' word, therefore, the plagues fell upon Egypt, until in the end a gang of powerless Hebrew slaves marched out as free men and women, having defeated the most powerful nation on earth.

God understands fear. Moses experienced fear. I myself feel the touch of fear every day. I am convinced that no living human being ever achieves complete freedom from it, but the difference between victory in life and long, drawn-out defeat rests in what you choose to do with the fear you feel. You can choose to obey fear or you can determine to move forward boldly in obedience to God in spite of it.

In 2007 a team from our church was preparing for a mission trip to Ukraine. At the same time, the son of a pastor in another state who seeks me out for pastoral oversight was raising funds for a mission trip to China. As he prayed, he felt God tell him to sow financially into our Ukraine trip and to trust God to multiply it back to him. Boldly and obediently, he sent us a very sacrificial gift for our trip to Ukraine in the face of a significant shortfall in his own fund-raising effort. Fear would have told him not to do it, but boldness moved him to obey. God did, in fact, multiply it back to him! He not only financed his own trip to China, but he took his newlywed bride with him. Boldness! It is nothing apart from risk.

Many believers fear to face the inner conditions of the heart that have been limiting or destroying their lives. The issues seem too dark, too big or too out of control. Exposure of personal flaws to a group or to a counselor can seem too great a risk. Powerlessness results. But a forward charge in boldness in spite of fear multiplies power. God meets you there and produces breakthrough for change.

In the summer of 1973 I had just completed my bachelor's degree and had come to the conclusion that God had called me to attend Fuller Theological Seminary. I applied, but it was late in the year. Acceptance to the program was a foregone conclusion, but they informed me that all available financial aid had already been allocated. I cried out to God concerning what clearly appeared to be a devastating setback in the face of overwhelming need. We had nothing. My wife of one year carried our first child in her womb and our families could give us no help at all. My heart sank.

Previously, I had been accepted to another seminary, affiliated with the denomination I belonged to at the time. A scholarship awaited me there, as well as a job for my wife, but the school was liberal in theology to the point of apostasy.

Through a beloved professor from my undergraduate days God intervened and directed me to Fuller Theological Seminary, but I had put it off too long and the obstacles appeared to be insurmountable. What to do? As I prayed, I believed God told me, *Burn your bridges.*

Immediately, I cancelled everything at the denominational school. No sooner had I obeyed and set my course than an obscure foundation I had never heard of granted me a full-ride scholarship to Fuller. I later learned that as a matter of policy the foundation granted the scholarship for one year only. My degree would require a three-year investment, but by the favor of God, the foundation granted me that scholarship each of my three years.

Having no idea how we might live with only enough money to get there and pay the first month's rent, I packed up my pregnant wife, loaded everything we owned into a U-Haul van and headed for Pasadena, California. I was young and terrified, but boldness in the face of fear opens the door for God to multiply power. We found an apartment on the first day, and my wife landed the first job she interviewed for, despite telling them she would have to quit when the baby came. Boldness in the Lord magnifies both your opportunities and your impact upon the world.

Winter 2007: Three young men from our church went to the cinema to watch a popular movie, pumped up by messages my son and I had been giving in which we encouraged our people to cross boundaries and minister God's power for healing in the marketplace, beyond the walls of the church. In the restroom after the movie, the Holy Spirit radiated from them with such power that a man they met there began to shake even before they had a chance to speak. Not understanding what had hit him, the man could only stammer, "Something big is about to happen! See? I'm shaking!" They offered to pray and watched the Holy Spirit shake him even harder, but it took boldness to cross a boundary in that most unlikely place. Boldness multiplies power for prophetic impact on the world around us.

Fall 2007: A group of young adults from our church prayed for words of knowledge concerning people they might meet in the marketplace before dispersing to find the people who matched the descriptions they had received. Specific impressions indicating gender, dress and conditions needing healing guided them as they went. At the supermarket two blocks away they found what they were looking for. Right there in the store, between loaves of bread and bottles of ketchup, several people received healing. One in particular demonstrated the relief she felt for the pain in her feet by dancing up and down the aisle pain-free. Boldness for prophetic impact! That woman's life will never be the same.

In American football, which halfback breaks through for the touchdown? The one who runs away for fear of being tackled? Or the one who waits a moment for his blockers to open the way and then boldly charges ahead? "For God has not given us a spirit of timidity, but of power and love and discipline" (2 Timothy 1:7).

Moses chose boldness in the face of weakness and God met him with power that made that one man more powerful than all the armies of Pharaoh.

Faithfulness and Household

The second force multiplier at work in Moses' life—and possibly the most important one—can be found in Numbers 12:7: "My servant Moses . . . is faithful in all My household."

Two key words work together here: *faithful* and *household.* God declared Moses faithful over His whole household. Moses was faithful to such a degree that in Exodus 32:10 he pled with God to spare the people when God Himself wanted to destroy them, even after God offered to make a nation out of him instead!

Who wins the race on the day of the track meet? Is it the one who trained when he felt like it and rested when he did not, or the one who showed up every day in the heat, the wind

107

and the rain? Is it the one who allowed his moods to determine his intensity, or the one who trained hard to the best of his ability in the face of every setback life could serve up?

In 1996 I served as part of the ministry team for a Catch the Fire conference held at Ed Roebert's church in South Africa, one of the largest congregations in that nation. As I absorbed the size of their congregation and the enormity of their interracial impact in that most racist of nations, I asked Ed how they had done it. His answer spoke to faithfulness over the household of God for the long haul. He quietly replied, "You stay, and you stay, and you stay."

I wonder how discouraged Moses felt when the first plague failed to turn Pharaoh's heart, or later when Pharaoh kept changing his mind as plague followed plague. It must have seemed like setback after setback. God sent ten plagues. Blood. Frogs. Gnats. Flies. Livestock disease. Boils. Hail. Locusts. Darkness. Death of the firstborn. Ten times Pharaoh hardened his heart, even after saying yes.

Later with his back to the sea, as the chariots approached, did Moses cry out in his heart, *When does it end? How many crises do I have to face? I can't take the stress anymore?* Certainly not! In the face of all that approaching destruction, regardless of the circumstances, he remained faithful and consistent in all God's household. He stood his ground, the sea parted and he won! God multiplied His power through Moses over and over again because Moses stood faithful.

Setbacks continued throughout the wilderness sojourn and still Moses stood. The people fainted and angered the Lord with their unfaithfulness and still Moses remained faithful. In every circumstance God came through and saved them because of Moses' faithfulness. Manna from heaven. Water from rocks. Bitter water made sweet. Enemies defeated.

Moses stood faithful over all God's *household.* The concept of the household goes a bit deeper than mere faithfulness. You and I might think of a household as three bedrooms, two baths and a garage, but that has never been God's definition.

In ancient times a household included a man, his wives, their children, their children's spouses and their children's children, as well as all their servants and their children. All these lived together either in a collection of tents or, in the case of a wealthy man, in a home that could include a great many rooms. For a rich man a household could number a hundred souls or more.

A household therefore indicates connection, a group of people bound together in love by covenant relationships. Moses never conceived of leading a gang of independent individuals to occupy their individual plots of land in isolation from one another. He set out to create a bonded people, living and working in oneness, ready to lay their lives down for one another, sharing an identity as the people of God.

Consistently and faithfully Moses cared for God's household, cultivating the relationships, defining the connections according to the revelation of God's Law. He sought to create a family of God in love, one household in Him. Until we can begin to think in terms of becoming a *household* of faith, we will remain limited in our power and impact on the world.

"Household" forms the arena in which we work out faithfulness in practical terms. Without faithfulness "household" cannot exist. On the other hand faithfulness cannot be expressed without a household in which to *be* expressed. "My servant Moses . . . is faithful in all My household." God calls us to be faithful both in the things of God and in relation to the people of God, not to be floating here and there, from church to church, fellowship to fellowship, but to enter into stable relationships, finding and doing what we have been called to do consistently for the Kingdom of God and for the sake of those with whom God has connected us.

This can be expressed in ways as simple as faithful attendance at a cell group meeting. It might be involvement in teaching the children in the Sunday school program at church and being careful to be there every week without fail. Those called to be intercessors can only create an effective team as they pursue unity with one another, which can be developed only by means of consistency. We grow in relationship to God as we grow in relationship with one another. Faithful over God's household! And where that faithfulness exists, God multiplies His power.

Household in the New Testament

In Acts 10, Cornelius and his entire household became believers, not one at a time but as a connected people. You see this same dynamic in Acts 16. Paul and Silas had been beaten with rods and cast into prison where they sat in the stocks worshiping. An earthquake shook the prison and all their chains fell off. The jailer feared they had escaped and prepared to take his own life, but Paul and Silas stopped him. Later, at the jailer's home, they preached the Gospel to his entire household:

> They said, "Believe in the Lord Jesus, and you will be saved, you and *your household*." And they spoke the word of the Lord to him together with all who were in his house. And he took them that very hour of the night and washed their wounds, and immediately he was baptized, he and all his household. And he brought them into his house and set food before them, and rejoiced greatly, having believed in God with his *whole household.*
>
> verses 31–34, emphasis mine

In both testaments, God Himself has a household over which and in which He calls each of us to be faithful. Paul wrote of "the household of God, which is the church of the living God, the pillar and support of the truth" (1 Timothy 3:15). Peter understood it as well. "For it is time for judgment to begin with the household of God" (1 Peter 4:17).

God has made each of us responsible for a portion of His household in the way we use the gifts He has given us (see

Romans 12; 1 Corinthians 12). Power multiplies in our individual lives when each of us exercises faithfulness in that portion of the household He has assigned to us. Apart from faithful connection to a specific local body of Christ in which we serve selflessly, there can be no full and powerful prophetic impact flowing from the Church to change the culture around us. Scattered, we diminish ourselves.

Few things have played a greater role in weakening the Body of Christ in our day than failure to understand both faithfulness and the concept of household. Our culture teaches us to exalt feelings as truth and self-fulfillment as our ideal. Under the guidance of our moods, faithfulness crumbles into inconsistency, while our focus on self destroys the kind of sacrifice needed to make a household work. Inconsistent and fragmented, the Body of Christ fails to impact the world with anything like the power Jesus intended for us. "That they may all be one . . . that the world may know." There in the oneness, in the establishment of a connected household visible to the world, lies true prophetic impact.

Summary

Moses practiced boldness in the face of fear, as well as faithfulness in all God's household. In these things God magnifies the expression of His power through us for the sake of those He wishes to save. In boldness and faithfulness over God's household, we become larger than the sum of our parts. When God sees boldness and faithfulness in relationship among His people He declares, "That looks like Me. This I can bless."

PART IV

ATMOSPHERES

8

Toward a Culture of Honor

Every truly prophetic community walks in oneness as a household of faith and shares a collective understanding of the status of its members as royalty. These things must be chosen in faithfulness, sustained and reinforced over time. Much of this involves cultivating a culture of honor. Here are just a few passages where the word *honor* appears.

First Peter 2:4–6 teaches us that we are living stones, choice and precious to God, together being built up as a temple of the Lord with Jesus Himself as the cornerstone. Verse 7 then states, "This precious value, then, is for you who believe." The word for "value" in the original Greek is *timé* (tih-*may*), most commonly translated as "honor," rather than "value." This precious "honor" is for us who believe. Although we have been rejected by the world, God has chosen and honored us as precious living stones for the temple in which He chooses to dwell. God Himself grants us this honor, value and position.

First Corinthians 12 begins with Paul's teaching concerning the gifts and manifestations of the Spirit and the operation of His power. This forms the context for verses 18–22, which speak of the function and necessity of every individual member of the Body. The issue of honor appears in the following verses:

> Those members of the body which we deem less honorable, on these we bestow more abundant honor, and our less presentable members become much more presentable, whereas our more presentable members have no need of it. But God has so composed the body, giving more abundant honor to that member which lacked [meaning value, place, worth], so that there may be no division in the body, but that the members may have the same care for one another. And if one member suffers, all the members suffer with it; if one member is *honored*, all the members rejoice with it. Now you are Christ's body, and individually members of it.
>
> verses 23–27, emphasis mine

Honor given to one edifies the many. When even the least honorable member receives honor, something precious multiplies for everyone.

The apostle wrote in Romans 12:10–11, "Be devoted to one another in brotherly love; give preference to one another in honor;" once again indicating value, place and worth, "not lagging behind in diligence, fervent in spirit, serving the Lord." In this case the gift of honor takes on overtones of coming under one another to lift and exalt.

Ephesians 6:2–3 applies the call to give honor to family relationships and points out its power to release blessing: "Honor your father and mother (which is the first commandment with a promise), so that it may be well with you, and that you may live long on the earth."

Peter carried it further. Honor must be granted not only to other believers and not only to parents, but to all people. "Honor all people, love the brotherhood, fear God, honor the king" (1 Peter 2:17). Assign to all people value, place and worth.

Like Paul, Peter brought it home to the family, and like Paul, he associated the giving of honor with a release of blessing. In the following passage, the gift of honor bestowed upon a wife directly affects the quality of a man's relationship with God.

> You husbands in the same way, live with your wives in an understanding way, as with someone weaker, since she is a woman; [referring to her weaker physical body only] and show her honor as a fellow heir of the grace of life, so that your prayers will not be hindered. To sum up, all of you be harmonious, sympathetic, brotherly, kindhearted, and humble in spirit; not returning evil for evil or insult for insult, but giving a blessing instead; for you were called for the very purpose that you might inherit a blessing.
>
> 1 Peter 3:7–9

Ascribing Worth and Value

If the word *honor* indicates the worth you ascribe to a person and the value you place on them, then to give honor is to demonstrate that value, to show it outwardly. One key of giving honor is to remind one another who we are and what we mean to our Father in heaven.

It has been said that yesterday's movies are today's parables, and one of my all-time favorites is *Braveheart*. At the battle of Stirling Bridge in 1297, according to the film, a rabble of Scottish farmers, ill-equipped and vastly outnumbered, faced an overwhelming force of Englishmen, well armed and trained and aided by "heavy horse." Terrified at the power arrayed before them, the Scots had begun to leave the battlefield. Enter William Wallace!

Spurring his horse back and forth before them, he delivered a marvelous exhortation that restored his terrified countrymen to their sense of identity and pride and strengthened them to fight for their freedom. "I see before me a whole army

117

of my countrymen gathered in defiance of tyranny!" Into that rabble of poorly trained peasant warriors who had no faith in themselves he injected honor and value, reminding them of the men they were. With courage and strength restored, they rushed the field that day to defeat an overwhelming force!

Honor is believing in people when they cannot believe in themselves. It is seeing the good in them and strengthening them for great exploits. Honor assigns value, and value imparts strength. For instance, a church member calls me at my office distraught because of raging emotions at the end of a string of devastating setbacks that have led him to feel as though he wants to abandon his faith. I listen and empathize, but then I begin to remind him who he is. "You've been with me a long time. I know who you are. The fact that you're on the phone with me right now says you're not going to abandon your faith. The tears you're shedding tell me you still care despite what you're saying." By the end of the conversation, he's laughing with me, restored, uplifted and ready to continue the fight. Honor!

The Gift of Honor as a Form of Love

The gift of honor is a form of love. According to 1 Corinthians 13:7, love "believes all things." For instance, Jesus recruited a group of fishermen to be His disciples, blue-collar workers despised by the religious establishment for their lack of education and for the fact that they came from Galilee. He called a tax collector, hated by his own people as a collaborator in the Roman occupation of their country. He even included a revolutionary who later betrayed Him. He saw what God had designed them to be and He honored them by giving them authority and position at His side in ministry. We might see this as the first step in the plan that "you also, as living stones, are being built up as a spiritual house for a holy priesthood, to offer up spiritual sacrifices acceptable to God through

Jesus Christ" (1 Peter 2:5). Again, "This precious value, then, is for you who believe" (verse 7). Value equals honor. Jesus believed in those He called. He honored something no one else could see and thereby released power into their lives that ultimately changed a world.

Later, Jesus supernaturally confronted a religious-spirited young man named Saul (who had presided over the stoning to death of Stephen, the deacon) as he traveled to Damascus intending to harm more believers. Jesus introduced Himself to Saul, gave instructions for his conversion and, in love, planted a sense of new destiny in his heart. As time passed, He changed his name to Paul and made him the greatest of all the apostles.

Paul's own attitude concerning himself remained one of humility: "For I am the least of the apostles, and not fit to be called an apostle, because I persecuted the church of God. But by the grace of God I am what I am" (1 Corinthians 15:9–10). God believed in and honored something He had deposited in Saul from the very beginning and then called it forth. Honor bestowed in grace activates people and releases the power of God for change.

I will tell you a secret. God has little interest in what you think of you, and He certainly has no interest in what you think of the one sitting next to you in the pew at church. In His incredible love, He is only interested in what *He* thinks of you, and what He thinks of you is rooted in honor, the worth He ascribes to you, the value He places on you, on your brother or sister and on any whom He has called.

Giving Preference to One Another

The apostle called us to give preference to one another in honor. In practice this means getting under and lifting one another to higher places.

In the summer of 1986 I sat on the front row in the Superdome in New Orleans next to Rice Broocks as Larry

Tomczak preached before a crowd of perhaps twenty-five thousand. Larry and Rice were close friends, approximately my own age, who worked together to oversee a network of churches. Rice, delighted and overflowing with godly pride, kept turning to me and exclaiming, "That's my man up there! Go Larry!" It struck me that thoughts like *That should be me up there* never entered his mind or heart. It simply delighted and deeply blessed him to see his friend doing well in a position of honor.

I remember feeling ashamed in my own heart because at that time in my life I was a tightly controlled and mostly concealed package of insecurities that fed jealousy, competition, ambition and arrogance. I knew that in Rice's place I would have been thinking, *That should be me up there.* I would have been functionally incapable of preferring a brother in honor.

Honor is never questioning, "Why wasn't *I* chosen?" Honor is rejoicing that your brother or your sister was chosen—"if one member is honored, all the members rejoice with it"—and getting under him or her to lift.

Honor so resonates the Father's love that it lifts the giver out of the spirit of poverty in which another's success, education, intelligence or gifting constitutes a threat or incites insecurity. When captivated by that love, you walk in a form of personal security that renders you immune to the need to bring others down in order to exalt yourself. You grow out of feeling as if you have been diminished by the honor, place or position given to others because you know that your Father loves *you* and that His storehouses hold plenty for all His children.

The Power of Honoring the Undeserving

In Luke 19, Jesus was passing through the streets, a crowd of people pressing close about him. Hanging around the fringes was a man named Zaccheus, a chief tax collector for the Romans, a collaborator cheating his own people as he helped maintain the oppressive Roman occupation of his native land. People hated him and would not allow him anywhere near Jesus. Too short to see over the crowd and inexorably drawn by the mercy and love he sensed in Jesus, he climbed up in a sycamore tree just to see Him pass by.

What happened next ignited a controversy in the religious establishment. Jesus invited Himself to Zaccheus's house for a meal. In our modern culture this means very little, but in the culture of Bible times Jesus had just bestowed a great honor, a tremendous gift of love, upon this unworthy little man. It was not that Jesus was hungry and could not find a restaurant. He deliberately and publicly chose to honor Zaccheus. The power of Jesus' gift of honor set him free to change.

> When they saw it, they all began to grumble, saying, "He has gone to be the guest of a man who is a sinner." Zaccheus stopped and said to the Lord, "Behold, Lord, half of my possessions I will give to the poor, and if I have defrauded anyone of anything, I will give back four times as much." And Jesus said to him, "Today salvation has come to this house, because he, too, is a son of Abraham."
>
> Luke 19:7–9

Jesus got under Zaccheus and lifted him. He bestowed a gift of honor in love upon one who richly deserved the condemnation his community heaped on him. This gift of honor awakened that thieving tax collector's dormant conscience and transformed his life. It strengthened him to do the right thing, to restore twice as much as Old Testament Law required in cases of fraud or theft. The impact of this act on the community that witnessed it had to be enormous.

We must therefore give honor both to the deserving and to the undeserving. Condemnation confronts sin by beating people down. Love confronts sin by reminding people who they are, by seeing in them the image of God with all of its value and then calling it forth. Love believes in the unbelievable.

Power Released

God has woven a principle into the fabric of the universe such that when we grant honor and value to others, power flows. You see it in 1 Corinthians 12, where the apostle first speaks of the power of spiritual gifts and then moves into all that mystery about honoring the least honorable. The context ties the giving of honor to the release of power. A prophetic people having a prophetic impact on the community around them must understand the connection between honor bestowed and power released.

You see it again in Ephesians 6:2–3 (previously noted) where the apostle connects honor of parents with subsequent wellbeing in life. This does not necessarily mean that adult children must trust untrustworthy or abusive parents or that we ought to come under them in any way. We are grown-ups, after all! But it does mean that we must assign value to them as human beings and treat them accordingly.

In the worst of parents God has planted something good, something created in His own image that can be valued and honored. When we grant such honor we pull down an inheritance of those good things into our own lives. I once knew a musician who had been raised by an abusive father. Even though she had long since forgiven his abuse, she struggled to honor him at any level, until one day she broke through to a recognition of the goodness of his gift of music. She began to honor him for it. Release of her own ministry in music followed.

Even more, I believe that in honoring our parents, good ones and bad ones, we draw down from heaven the inheritance of Jesus Himself because He first honored His heavenly Father as we have been called to honor our earthly parents.

A Personal Testimony

Some years ago I pulled away from my mother and father for a time because of wounding and dysfunction in our family system that I could no longer overcome. We have always been a good family, but we remain a long way from perfect! Because I could not find my way to wholeness within the power of the family system, I needed space to heal and grow until the system no longer had power over me.

It took time, but I prayed it through and received good healing with the help of some very good counseling. Afterward God told me to reengage with my father in particular. Healed in heart and soul, I did so. I honored him and I continue to honor him. After that honoring, my church began to change for the good and our finances began to prosper. After my gift of honor my current publisher, one of the best, began publishing my books and people began regarding me as a reliable prophet—an appellation with which I remain uncomfortable. Honor pulled down from heaven the massive inheritance my parents had stored up for me in their lives and ministries. Honor releases blessing and power.

I graduated from Fuller Seminary in 1976 and took a position in a Methodist church as youth pastor. I was young, wet behind the ears and a bit handicapped in the wisdom department. As sometimes happens in the Methodist system, just a year later the annual conference moved my senior pastor to another congregation and sent in a replacement. The replacement came from a situation in which he had known tremendous favor, freedom and authority. Blind to the need to take time to listen to the people and win their hearts before making significant changes, he came assuming the same level of favor, freedom and authority he had exercised in his previous position.

Because I was the remaining staff member, people began lining up to complain to me about him. There was even talk of asking the district superintendent to remove him. I was in over my head, unprepared by age or experience to navigate this tricky stream and not a little flattered at the attention paid me.

I soon received a call from a seasoned and godly pastor in a neighboring community inviting me to lunch. I include his name here for the honor I wish to pay him. When we had finished lunch, Reverend Al Vom Steeg took me to his office where he assumed an imposing position of authority behind his very large desk. Leaning across it and fixing me with a penetrating gaze, he carefully and deliberately stated, "How you honor your senior pastor now will determine the way your associates treat you for the rest of your career." He waited a moment to see if the words had sunk in and then quickly crossed the room to drop to his knees before the couch to pray, looking over his shoulder at me as if to say, "What are you still doing there, young fool?" Humbled, I quickly joined him.

Upon my return I began to do everything I could to become my senior pastor's advocate. I tried to comprehend the direction in which he wanted to move the congregation and I sought to understand his heart. When the complainers came to seek my ear, I did what I could to interpret him to them, to point out the good that I perceived and knew. In honor, I tried to lift him up and smooth his way. In the end, he remained the beloved pastor of that church for more than twenty years and multiplied its membership significantly. I believe I played at least some small role in establishing his position there. My reward? I learned more from him than from any other senior pastor I served under in the early years of my ministry. Honor releases power and blessing.

For a brief time in the early 1990s I served as the executive pastor of a very large church known for its emphasis on worship. I had not been there very long when one Sunday morning a young woman began dancing in the sweetest and most lovely way back and forth across the front of the sanctuary. I loved it. To my surprise and dismay, my senior pastor did not. He told me, "That's twelve thousand pairs of eyes following her back and forth. You go down there and tell her to stop that or I'll embarrass her."

I disagreed. But giving honor to my senior pastor meant first that I had no choice, and second that I had to do it in a loving way that would not dishonor or shame her. Third, it meant I had to do it in a way that did not reflect badly on my senior pastor. I had to get under and lift. I could think of no approach that would not cause wounding, so I spoke as gently and lovingly as I could, explaining that my senior pastor simply did not want to allow dancing at the front of the sanctuary. At the back would be perfectly acceptable. I refused to disparage him and I tried my best not to wound her. Rendering honor can often be a difficult thing, but I know that I have reaped the fruit of the honor I gave in the freedom and the glory of the worship my congregation today enjoys.

Many of us would do well to ask ourselves this question: *Why I am still stuck in a place that is less than the promise of God?* The answer might be that you need to grasp the principle of honor, "that it may be well with you."

The Testimony of Scripture in the Life of David

You see this principle illustrated in the Old Testament in David's life. In contrast to David, King Saul lived as a child in a man's body, ever compromising the Lord's command for the sake of urgency and unable to take full responsibility for his failures. Threatened by David's anointing and bitter over his own failure and foolishness, he grew jealous. He drove David from his court into the wilderness and spent years trying to kill him, yet even at the risk of his own life David refused to dishonor Saul in any way.

In 1 Samuel 24 David and his men concealed themselves in a cave. Saul came hunting David and entered the cave to relieve himself. In the dark recesses of the cave David's men urged him to take this opportunity to strike his enemy down. In honor David refused to lift his hand against one he called "the Lord's anointed." Instead, as Saul squatted in the darkness, David sneaked up and cut off a piece of the edge of his robe, but even this was more than his conscience could bear. He therefore presented himself in the open before Saul and repented.

Saul's line died out and his dynasty never took root, but David became king of all Israel. From his royal line comes Jesus. Honor, even if only in the form of refusal to *dis*honor, releases power and blessing. God set up His Kingdom to function on the gift of honor, assigning value to all men and women and treating them accordingly.

A Culture of Honor

Culture is the "soup" in which we live. It surrounds us and permeates us. We sense it every day. We hear it, see it and soak in it. At the most subconscious levels it teaches us how to speak, think, feel and function. We instinctively do, feel and value what the culture teaches us because it becomes part of us. These cultural ways feel self-evidently right. We treat one another according to the norms of the culture around us. Our attitudes reflect the atmosphere that conditions us. We speak with an accent depending on the culture in which we grew up.

A truly prophetic church must cultivate a culture of honor among its members such that every new person catches the spirit of it simply by being immersed in it. We must cultivate a culture that teaches all its members to honor and value one another. As that culture takes root, you instinctively sense when you have stepped out of line and failed to assign value to people, to get under and lift. It feels wrong to you when you fail to rejoice when one of your brothers or sisters receives a promotion. Your stomach churns when negative talk begins to cloud the clarity of the Spirit with the fog of accusation and criticism. We become those "who because of practice have their senses trained to discern good and evil" (Hebrews 5:14).

The culture of honor must become second nature to us. As it does, we will see growth, people being saved, lives prospering, finances changing, bodies being healed and more. In a culture of honor we find hope for redemption, and hope draws the masses in a way condemnation never can.

Once established in the Church, the culture of honor carries over into the workplace, the home, the neighborhood and all our other dealings. Prophetic impact is made in such a way. Things change.

Speaking personally, before the culture of honor can truly take hold, I must grasp the truth that Father God has honored and loved me. It must become real to me that I have been adopted as His son through His sacrifice of Jesus on the cross, that He has made me royalty and granted me an inheritance in His house. If I can absorb this and truly understand it, then honor will flow freely from me to lift others. The culture of honor begins with understanding the Father's love for you, His choosing of you, His gift of favor to you and His choice of you for position and honor as a living stone in a holy temple.

If we can develop a culture of honor in the Church, we will see a release of all the power we have ever longed for, and by it we will prophetically impact and change our world. But our sense of wonder will not derive from miracles and demonstrations of power. At the heart of it—filling us with awe—will be miraculous levels of love and honor.

9

Faith, Honor and Atmosphere

I n 1967 I was sixteen years old. The high school I attended had 180 students, sophomores through seniors. The town? Maybe 2000. My father pastored the leading church in the community and I led the only rock band. And everybody knew everything about everybody.

So one day I had to visit the dentist. After he shot me up with a needle at least a foot long and waited for my mouth to become useless, he filled it with all kinds of mechanical stuff and then began to say things. "I know where you were last Friday night. You were at that kegger, weren't you?"

"Anngggh!" I growled.

"I know about you and that little blonde girl." Actually, he did not, despite the fact that I wished I really had a little blonde girl in my life.

"Anngggh!" I growled once more.

Not yet satisfied with my level of physical and emotional discomfort, he continued. "Wrecked your daddy's car, didn't you?"

True. But I tried to answer anyway in an effort to shut him up. "Annggh!"

"I know what you guys do in that rock band. You want to be one of those dirty hippies, don't ya?"

True again, but to my teenage mind the man was a jerk. "Anngggh!"

Really, I could say nothing to change his opinion of me. Our little town had everybody pegged. If you lived there all your life you would be thought of in the same way at age forty as you were viewed at fourteen. The town would never allow you out of the box. Nothing really good would ever be expected of you, and you would never be permitted a fair chance to respond to rumors and put-downs. As long as you lived in that community, you might as well have a mouth full of dentist tools and Novocain for all the chances you would be given to alter perceptions of yourself.

Even after high school, when I came home from college for Christmas and summer vacations, the negative expectations persisted. I worked underground in the hard rock mines of north Idaho during those vacations in order to make money for school. During lunch break one day in my third summer, one of the old miners learned that I was in college and intoned matter-of-factly with not a little contempt, "You'll be back. Yep! You'll be back," meaning that just like all the other hometown boys, I would be nothing but a miner all my life. He felt diminished by my advancement, expected nothing of me and wanted nothing for me but the status quo.

Small Town Nazareth

Jesus grew up in Nazareth, a small town much like mine. Everybody knew Him and they had Him in a box. Among Jewish people in Bible times, bloodlines mattered. Identity and heritage came down through the paternal line and defined both personal identity and place in the community.

One whose paternity could be questioned stood in a lower place than others. Witness the lengthy genealogies included in Scripture! Lineage meant honor, place and position.

Joseph was not Jesus' father and everyone in Nazareth knew it. They had no idea who His true father might be, but no one spoke out loud about it, at least not where anyone could hear. Gossip always works best behind closed doors. The community therefore quietly despised Jesus from the day Mary and Joseph brought Him home, in spite of the biblical affirmation that He grew in favor with God and men (see Luke 2:52). Small towns reek of such contradictions.

On top of this, they had known Jesus when His diapers needed changing. They had seen Him as a toddler just learning to walk. They had watched Him as He trudged off to Hebrew school to learn Scripture along with every other child in town. They had seen him hot, sweaty and covered with sawdust as He labored in the carpenter shop.

He grew up and became a man until, at last, the time came for Him to leave and begin His public ministry. Before long, reports of miracles began flowing into Nazareth. The blind received sight! The lame walked! Sick people recovered! He cast out demons with a word! Huge crowds followed Him everywhere He went. "Disciples?! Jesus has disciples?! *That* Jesus?!"

And then He returned home. Sabbath custom in the synagogue allowed for Him to expound on the Torah, and so with His disciples gathered around Him He took His turn at teaching. The people of Nazareth who thought they knew Him so well took offense, questioning the miracles and disparaging His wisdom, but the real blow came as the gospel of Mark reports:

> "Is not this the carpenter, the son of Mary, and brother of James and Joses and Judas and Simon? Are not His sisters here with us?" And they took offense at Him. Jesus said to them, "A prophet is not without honor except in his hometown and

131

among his own relatives and in his own household." And He could do no miracle there except that He laid His hands on a few sick people and healed them.

6:3–5

Deep-seated refusal to grant honor, not unbelief, prevented Jesus from exercising His power in His own hometown. Note verse 3, "They took offense at Him," and verse 4, "A prophet is not without honor except in his hometown and among his own relatives and in his own household." If unbelief had anything to do with it, dishonor stood at the root of it. *Failure to honor equals unbelief,* which is why in the parallel passage in Matthew 13:57–58 Jesus Himself cited dishonor as the barrier and then Matthew commented, "because of their unbelief."

They called Him "the son of Mary" at a time when people knew a man as the son of his father through whom lineage and identity came. Sons of Zebedee. Sons of Abraham. Sons of Jacob. Lineage and heritage flowed through the father's line. To speak of a man as the son of his mother was an ugly insult. It implied that his mother had been immoral and that he therefore had no value, no place, no heritage. When they called Jesus the son of Mary, they meant to bring Him down and rob Him of all dignity.

For this son-of-His-mother's presumption to rise to such an exalted place, wielding the power of God and gathering disciples, they took small-town offense. His power and wisdom diminished their sense of themselves. Nothing erodes the spirit of honor faster or more completely than the spirit of offense. Failure to honor constitutes unbelief.

Honor and the Release of Miracles

Not a church exists anywhere without a large number of its members needing miracles of healing. Cancers. Heart problems. Deafness. Bad knees. Backs. Diabetes. Hepatitis. Asthma. Viruses that refuse to go away. The list is endless and medical science has not yet advanced so far in healing us as we would like to believe. Even in the developed nations of the world we desperately need the intervention of God, and we see it from time to time in many renewal churches, but we need more. We need it in the Church and we need it for our ministries in the world, in our workplaces, in our neighborhoods and in our families.

The most important reason we see only sporadic miraculous ministry has little to do with unbelief. God does not hold His mercy hostage to our lack of mental or emotional certainty. Doubt has never held the power to restrain His mercy. God is too big for, "Sorry! You needed five pounds of faith for that and you have only four!" Some of the most significant healing miracles that have happened in my own ministry have come about in spite of my personal doubt. In such cases "unbelief" does not equate with emotional uncertainty. Obedient action constituted "belief" in spite of inward doubt. Inwardly doubting, I moved forward in obedience and God responded.

Lack of honor, however, does hold the power to restrain God's hand. This includes the honor we fail to ascribe to God, but even more, it includes the honor we fail to grant to one another. In an atmosphere of honor, power flows. Where people withhold honor from one another, God restrains His hand.

Jesus was more gifted. He had achieved a position in the world to which they could not attain and had been granted wisdom and knowledge they could only scarcely comprehend. He performed miracles they could not begin to replicate. The people of Nazareth took offense because Jesus stood above them. This pervasive atmosphere of dishonor in Nazareth restrained Jesus' hand. Power will not flow in an atmosphere of dishonor. Dishonor of one another constitutes a form of unbelief in God Himself. By contrast, *honor creates an atmosphere in which there is no impediment to the flow of power.*

Honor for one another actually constitutes a form of faith in the God who created each of us in His own image. Honor ascribes value, place and position to a person. The people of Nazareth wanted to strip Jesus of value, place and position so they could feel better about themselves. *We know His mother, brothers and sisters, but we don't know who His father is. He's nothing! Who does Jesus think He is?* Dishonor blocks the power of God. Honor releases it.

What I Have Witnessed

In 1979 I joined my parents' ministry, Elijah House, in Coeur d'Alene, Idaho, where I served for a time counseling, developing materials and teaching. Despite our best efforts and prayers, there never seemed to be a sense of unity. I often found myself in the midst of a maelstrom of negativity and statements like, "It should be done *this* way! If John would only listen to *me!*" The atmosphere reeked of grumbling and complaining. Not surprisingly, we continually struggled financially. It was not that my father failed as a leader, although he functions more as a visionary than a corporate manager. The problem lay in the people and in their own bitter roots.

A couple of years later, I left Elijah House to plant a church while remaining on the board and continuing as part of the teaching staff. Finally, in 1991 I moved to Denver, Colorado, where I remain. Throughout all that time I kept hearing reports of interpersonal problems, criticisms, complaints and financial struggles at Elijah House.

Eventually, the ministry hired a new chief executive officer and appointed my brother Mark as spiritual director. The atmosphere at Elijah House completely changed. Between my brother and the new CEO, honor came into the mix. They loved the people who worked at Elijah House and blessed them. They listened to them, pointed out their gifts and strengths and lifted them up.

In such an atmosphere of honor, finances began to turn. It seemed to me as an observer that more people received more healing more quickly because the counseling there became more effective. Elijah House products began to sell at a faster pace than ever before. New revelation began to flow and the ministry expanded as a true team atmosphere took root and grew.

All it required was the gift of honor pursued consistently enough to become the culture of the corporation. I have visited churches and ministries in which an atmosphere of faith filled the gathered believers, but where I nevertheless saw nothing happen. On the other hand, I have never visited a ministry or fellowship in which an atmosphere of honor predominated where glorious things failed to unfold. Never have I placed a more important goal before the people of my own congregation than cultivating an atmosphere of honor in which the power of God can move freely and without hindrance.

Making War on the Critical Spirit

We must make war on the critical spirit that belittles and deprives people of value. That spirit operates in two arenas of life. One of them affects the way you think of yourself.

Dishonoring Yourself

I have an education—seven years of full-time higher education after high school at two of the best institutions in the country. Education has given me much useful knowledge and put wonderful tools in my box. But knowledge does not release the power of the Holy Spirit. Knowledge does not make miracles. The Holy Spirit of God dwelling in the believer does that. Spiritual gifting does that. The call of God does that.

But too many Christians hold a fundamentally dishonoring view of themselves, which stands at odds with the reality that each of us has been filled with the Holy Spirit and empowered by Him. Some in my congregation, for instance, know that they have not acquired my level of education or my years of experience. In comparing themselves to what they believe I have, they feel wrongly diminished by the deficits they perceive in themselves.

Things like education and experience ought to be respected and honored, but at an emotional level too many refuse to believe that they have been given any gifts for ministry, that God speaks to them in any way, that they have anything at all to contribute or that God can or would choose to move through them in power. Why? Because in some cases they do not believe they have what I have. The truth is that many of my people exercise greater gifts than my own that need to be honored and respected, not hidden or minimized. If I have just described you, then know that you have dishonored both yourself and that which God has created in you.

An atmosphere of dishonor has infused every church I have ever known until the one I now pastor in just the same way it infects the culture around us. This begins in each individual heart with your own ungodly beliefs concerning yourself and with your own denial of how desperately and infinitely God loves and favors you. This dishonor of self then flows out into what you think, feel and expect of your brothers and sisters in the Lord. You stand in criticism of yourself and it causes you to be critical, minimizing and dishonoring of others.

Dishonoring Others

There are certain people who have been in your life for a very long time. You know where they hurt, where they struggle and what they have done in past years. You know their children and how well or badly they have reared them. You have witnessed their mistakes. You see their character flaws and perhaps you have suffered personally because of them. As a result, you fail to see or affirm their gifts, their progress, their growth, the changes God has been making. The prophet has no honor in his own hometown and so God restrains His hand because honor has been withheld.

A friend of mine has a problem with repeated outbursts of anger. Each time he allows an outburst to happen, he hurts people and destroys their trust in him. If I were to allow that character flaw to become the lens through which I see the whole picture with respect to him, do you suppose I might have a problem expecting God to move in power when he prays for people? Would that not be a form of dishonor? Is it possible that I might have trouble honoring his gift of teaching? Would I find myself suspicious of his gift of mercy? Certainly! But then I would be part of shutting off the flow of power for miracles in the whole fellowship of which I am a part.

Assigning Significance

A culture of honor assigns value and significance to every member of that culture. Hebrews 10:22–25 says:

> Let us draw near with a sincere heart in full assurance of faith, having our hearts sprinkled clean from an evil conscience and our bodies washed with pure water. Let us hold fast the confession of our hope without wavering, for He who promised is faithful; and let us consider how to stimulate one another to love and good deeds, not forsaking our own assembling together, as is the habit of some, but encouraging one another; and all the more as you see the day drawing near.

On the one hand, the apostle definitely exhorted his readers to stop skipping church—you cannot encourage anyone if you are not present to do it—but the real vision this passage sets before us is the cultivation of an atmosphere of honor among God's people that encourages, uplifts and stimulates all its members.

My parents grew up in a culture that taught them that if you gave a child a compliment he or she would get a "big head" and be filled with pride. Obviously, one would not wish to infuse a child with the sin of pride. Therefore, if you wanted the child to do better, you offered criticism in order to inspire greater effort.

Given my rebellious nature, this meant that my parents and I were headed for a train wreck from day one. I came forth from my mother's womb profoundly self-centered, functionally incapable of consideration for anyone but myself. For example, at the age of seven I asked for an electric train and when my father told me we could not afford it, I told him to sell the family car. Each year my sister saved up her money to buy Christmas presents for others while I spent mine on myself and then had nothing to give.

Hoping to inspire me to change, my parents responded to my selfishness by heaping criticism and condemnation on me, but the more criticism and condemnation they employed, the more emotionally disturbed and wounded I became. The more emotionally disturbed and wounded I became, the more I fell into a prison of dark self-centeredness. I really needed someone to see into my true heart and find a way to stimulate me to love and good deeds through honor rather than condemnation. This was true of me as a child and it remains true of us as adults.

Had they really noticed me crying as I watched Lassie come running home in *Lassie's Odyssey* on television at the age of five or six, they might have seen my tender heart and blessed it to life to overcome the tendency to self-focus. Perhaps they could have connected with the fact that I became the leader of the children of the neighborhood whenever I was in the mix. They could have built upon that, affirming the leadership gift, to help me lead for others' sakes. Any number of honoring and affirming approaches to shaping my character would have saved me years of torment in later life as I fought to overcome the prison of self in which I felt so trapped. I would have been stimulated to love and good deeds. For the record, we have since discussed and resolved this issue in healing in our family system.

Encouragement Is the Key

We accomplish this kind of stimulation primarily through one word in Hebrews 10:25—*encouragement*. Not dishonor. We must seek to discern the honorable thing in one another and then pour the Spirit of God out upon it. Probably the most essential element in creating a culture of honor is the simple gift of encouragement.

At any given time, for instance, I carry half a dozen young adults in my heart who have found themselves in the midst of trying to figure out what to do with life. In many cases they have become discouraged for lack of direction. Many have assumed that education beyond high school is impossible or that they lack the intelligence to pursue higher education. They have heard this all their lives from parents, teachers and peers. In a culture of condemnation I might think of them as losers and fools, grunts, lower class—and they would believe me because they already feel this way about themselves.

By contrast, in a culture of honor I want to confront them with their abilities and their potential. I see these things by the natural eye as well as by the gift of the Holy Spirit. In short, I believe in them and I make certain they know it. I see what God has planted in them and I try to call it forth, challenging them to stretch themselves and grow. I encourage them in their intelligence and I tell them how proud I am of the young men and women they are becoming. I tell them that they *can*. Some of them might have less knowledge than I do but their gifts in certain areas exceed my own. I speak these things into their lives. In a culture of honor, their capacity to do greater things than I have done fills me with joy, not with threat.

What Do We "Consider"?

Take another look at Hebrews 10:24: "Let us consider how to stimulate one another to love and good deeds." To "consider" something means to spend time thinking about it, pondering it and working it over in your mind and heart. Whatever you spend time considering, pondering and working on in your mind and heart will sooner or later come out of your mouth and infect others.

As a general rule, the enemy of our soul sees what we have set as a goal and moves to stop it because he knows that if we succeed, real power will flow from heaven. When I first began to speak of a culture of honor among our people, a few of my people almost immediately began to do, think and say some really foolish and hurtful things. Promises were broken. Outbursts of anger wounded people. Authoritative and misleading statements were made concerning programs or events that those making the statements had no authority to make. In each case I had to clean up the mess.

In the face of this, I suddenly found myself being tested. My mind and heart wanted to dwell on—"consider"—the failures and offenses I kept hearing about. I felt defiled and frustrated at being forced to deal with them. The more I thought about them, the more my sense of offense grew and the more I had to struggle with it. Before long this growing sense of offense began to come out of my mouth to infect my wife and a few others in whom I confided. What I consider in my heart ultimately expresses in words that affect the lives of others and erode the culture of honor God has called me to nurture.

By contrast, in a culture of honor we seek the "God things" in the lives of others. We direct our hearts and minds to consider these because, if we do, then ultimately those positive things will come out of our mouths and contribute to the culture of honor. How do I call out the best in my brother or sister? I want to see beyond offense and touch that sister's heart for the good. How do I do that? I see a gift of prayer, healing, prophecy, compassion or service in that brother. What can I do to affirm and activate that? How do I give encouragement and so strengthen the hand of God?

Paul had it right in Philippians 4:8: "Finally, brethren, whatever is true, whatever is honorable, whatever is right, whatever is pure, whatever is lovely, whatever is of good repute, if there is any excellence and if anything worthy of praise, dwell on these things." Why? Because Jesus said that the mouth speaks out of that which fills the heart. On what do your heart and mind dwell?

"It's Not There!"

In 2008 a major conference came to my city on how to do signs, wonders and healings. Top international leaders came to teach us what they knew. To my dismay, God in His sovereignty kept me from attending and even prevented me from advertising it in my church. The circumstances that stood in the way formed a bizarre complex of events and situations that upset and confused me. I needed understanding.

God answered clearly, *It's not there*, and I began to ponder what He meant. Now I believe I know. What my people and I needed would not be found in notebooks filled with teaching. The methods and the how-to's would not take us there. We would not find it in the impartation of gifts bestowed through the laying on of hands by some great leader. In reality, we already had all that. We had been over-trained and over-filled for a very long time.

The missing ingredient for us could only be found in cultivating and creating an atmosphere of honor that would constitute an atmosphere of faith. In such an atmosphere we honor what God honors and respect what God respects. In honor we trust Him (trust equals faith) to cause our brothers and sisters to grow and to use them for glory from the least to the greatest. In a culture of honor I come to believe His incredible love for me and for you and I respect the gifts He has placed in us both.

Through the Least of These

Some years ago a group of seminary students visited my church as part of a class study project that included a presentation of our philosophy of worship. Knowing that a single image can communicate more than many words, I prepared a video of a Sunday service, complete with clips of ministry time. After the showing, one of the students rather carefully raised a question, wishing not to offend in any way: "Pardon me, I don't mean to be offensive, but did I see handicapped people there?"

I replied, "Yes, you did." The clips of ministry time included several of our impaired people ministering in prayer and laying on of hands. I told the class that we instinctively tend to think that the Holy Spirit cannot move as easily or powerfully through someone with slurred speech or whose mental capacity is diminished as He can through someone whose physical and mental capacities are intact. I let them know that I teach our people that the Holy Spirit can move just as easily through someone with a disability as through a person whose mind and body are completely healthy.

They just looked at me as what I said sank in. Seminary can be a very performance-oriented environment that exalts intelligence as a form of anointing and power, but if they really heard what I was saying, then they absorbed the meaning of honor. A culture of honor believes in the least of its members. It actually builds faith because it looks past the man or the woman and into the heart of the God who loves them, created them and uses them.

In Jesus' hometown they belittled and dishonored Him. As a result, He could do no miracles there. When we belittle anyone for any reason, we create and feed an atmosphere of unbelief. Honor nurtures an atmosphere in which God releases power because honor given is a form of love.

> For God so loved the world, that He gave His only begotten Son, that whoever believes in Him shall not perish, but have eternal life. For God did not send the Son into the world to judge the world, but that the world might be saved through Him.
>
> John 3:16–17

Here is the heart of God. When we give honor to one another we nurture a gift of faith in the God who created those to whom we grant honor. Do this, and we will see the miracle power of God released through us upon a needy world. This would be the kind of prophetic impact that would send ripples and shock waves through this post-Christian culture in which we live.

10

Increase Our Faith

I nearly chose not to write a chapter addressing the issue of faith in general. So many have written so much about faith over the last few decades, it would hardly seem necessary, and yet so much of what has been written has been out of balance or simply wrong. The most foundational of the erroneous teachings prevalent in the Body of Christ presents faith as if it were some kind of power in itself that could somehow be measured as a quantity and employed to accomplish the desires of its holder. As a result millions of Christians have been taught a magical view of faith. In other words they have faith in their faith as opposed to having real faith in the object of our faith—the one true God.

So what is faith? The most fundamental meaning of the word *faith* in the original Greek of the Bible is "trust." Simple trust. Rested trust. God built us from the beginning for that kind of relationship with Him. It should be our native element. At the foundation of any prophetic people must be a pervasive, contagious atmosphere of trust.

The Sin of Adam

The root of the sin of Adam in partaking of the forbidden fruit was a breach of trust, an act of unbelief. Created in God's image, Adam and Eve had been made like Him, but the serpent deceived them and led them to disbelieve what they had been given at the core of their natures. The serpent convinced Eve that in order to become like God she must partake of the forbidden fruit. She did so and then led Adam to partake as well. In that act, they shattered their trust in the God who made them.

Ever since that day we have inherited the fruit of their trespass in our inability to truly trust God and find rest in Him. Just look at how frequently Jesus confronted the disciples with what He called "little faith" or "the littleness of your faith." Faith means "to trust" or "to have confidence in." Do we have confidence in God? Do we really trust Him? Have we really understood the nature of faith?

Faith has often been misunderstood as a power or force that makes things happen as if we could move the world by getting enough of it or by striving after it. God has a different idea. He intends faith to define a state of relationship with Him in which we rest completely in His loving and perfect care so that no matter what we face or what befalls us in life we stand confidently in Him.

This kind of rest can present difficulties for us because distrust of God and lack of confidence in Him lie at the very heart of our sin nature and form the core of the very first offense. We inherit it, generation by generation, from our first parents, Adam and Eve. But the last Adam, Jesus, restores faith to us and makes it the key to our salvation and wholeness. "For by grace you have been saved *through faith*; and that not of yourselves, it is the gift of God; not as a result of works, so that no one may boast" (Ephesians 2:8–9, emphasis mine).

Trust connects us with God's love that saves us. The love never varies. It was there all the time. The problem lies in our ability to trust and experience that love. Faith bridges that gap. All of my life I have asked for more faith. I have come to understand that I have really been asking for a healed relationship with Father God through Jesus founded upon a growing and ever more simple trust in Him.

Jesus said,

> "Why are you worried about clothing? Observe how the lilies of the field grow; they do not toil nor do they spin, yet I say to you that not even Solomon in all his glory clothed himself like one of these. But if God so clothes the grass of the field, which is alive today and tomorrow is thrown into the furnace, will He not much more clothe you? You of little faith!"
>
> Matthew 6:28–30

In the absence of such trust, we struggle unnecessarily in an atmosphere of fear. A prophetic people making an impact on the world around them exude a radiant aura of rested faith and trust. When we believe and live what we say, then others believe what we live and say.

> Behold, there arose a great storm on the sea, so that the boat was being covered with the waves; but Jesus Himself was asleep. And they came to Him and woke Him, saying, "Save us, Lord; we are perishing!" He said to them, "Why are you afraid, you men of little faith?" Then He got up and rebuked the winds and the sea, and it became perfectly calm.
>
> Matthew 8:24–26

"Little faith" means they had little trust. In the absence of real trust, every storm of life knocks us off balance, even when we know that He has carried us through every tempest we ever faced in the past and brought impossible good out of each of them. But mistrust lies at the heart of our sin nature, woven into every aspect of our fallen selves. This explains why unbelief can seem so difficult to root out and overcome.

Gazing into the Face of Jesus

I frequently speak of absorbing the nature and character of Jesus. The heart of His nature and character is love infusing every intent of the heart and every action taken. But we must add another dimension to our quest to be Christlike and call it "trust." Jesus trusted the Father perfectly, without flaw or variation. If Jesus heals the breach between us and Father God, restoring the relationship, does not trust lie at the heart of it? If Jesus conquers our sin and changes us from glory to glory as we look into His face, then does not foundational trust in Father God form the basis of our victory and transformation? And how can a people be prophetic in their impact if they cannot communicate rested trust in the God they proclaim?

Peter

Most of us know the story of Peter walking on the water. Jesus walked toward the disciples across the windblown surface of the lake with its waves and white caps and commanded Peter to come to Him. As Peter obeyed, he found himself walking on the water just like Jesus.

> But seeing the wind, he became frightened, and beginning to sink, he cried out, "Lord, save me!" Immediately Jesus stretched out His hand and took hold of him, and said to him, "You of little faith, why did you doubt?" When they got into the boat, the wind stopped.
>
> Matthew 14:30–32

Fear of the storm and a sense of the turbulent water beneath him overcame the momentary trust that had held him up. The storm appeared to be bigger than Jesus. The moment that assessment entered his heart, he sank. Little trust. "Why didn't you trust Me?"

The Disciples' Failure

The issue of trust appears again in Matthew 17 when the disciples brought to Jesus the boy possessed by a demon that the disciples could not cast out. In verse 17 when they cried to understand their inability, "Jesus answered and said, 'You unbelieving and perverted generation.'" *Unbelieving* comes from the same root word as *faith* in the original Greek with the negative added. The word *perverted* means that sin has destroyed the gift God gave Adam at the beginning and has twisted what He designed us to be. God designed us to rest in the perfect care of a perfect Father.

In exasperation, Jesus therefore lamented, "'How long shall I be with you? How long shall I put up with you? Bring him here to Me.' And Jesus rebuked him, and the demon came out of him, and the boy was cured at once. Then the disciples came to Jesus privately and said, 'Why could we not drive it out?' And He said to them, 'Because of the littleness of your faith,'" by which He meant their lack of real trust in the goodness and care of the Father God, "'for truly I say to you, if you have faith the size of a mustard seed, you will say to this mountain, "Move from here to there," and it will move; and nothing will be impossible to you'" (Matthew 17:17–20). Mountain-moving speaks of impact. A prophetic people must walk in an atmosphere of genuine faith.

A Centurion's Faith

In Matthew 8 Jesus met the centurion whose servant lay at home deathly ill.

But the centurion said, "Lord, I am not worthy for You to come under my roof, but just say the word, and my servant will be healed. For I also am a man under authority, with soldiers under me; and I say to this one, 'Go!' and he goes, and to another, 'Come!' and he comes, and to my slave, 'Do this!' and he does it." Now when Jesus heard this, He marveled and said to those who were following, "Truly I say to you, I have not found such great faith with anyone in Israel."

Matthew 8:8–10

The centurion *trusted* the authority he saw in Jesus. Therein lies the definition of faith. More than this, he recognized the authority that flows from faith. As a soldier, the centurion understood that no battle can be won unless the soldier trusts his commander. Trust issues in obedience. The centurion saw Jesus' authority and understood that it flowed from faith and trust in His Commander.

A Woman Made Well

Matthew 9:20–22 contains another story of faith:

And a woman who had been suffering from a hemorrhage for twelve years, came up behind Him and touched the fringe of His cloak; for she was saying to herself, "If I only touch His garment, I will get well." But Jesus turning and seeing her said, "Daughter, take courage; your faith has made you well." At once the woman was made well.

We must not misunderstand this woman's faith as some kind of force or power in itself, but rather as trust in what she had seen in Jesus. True faith manifests as rested trust in His mercy and faithfulness. She knew what she had seen and sensed and she trusted Jesus enough to risk public exposure of her defilement under Old Testament Law in order to access it.

As I stated earlier, too many of us make the mistake of having faith in our own faith rather than in Jesus, the object of our faith. The power flowed from Jesus, not from the woman's faith. Faith served as the mechanism that brought her to Him, the bridge that connected her to the experience of His love and mercy. We must trust in the goodness of our God and rest in the power that flows from Jesus.

The Basis of Relationship

The Pharisees made submission to the Law the focus of their relationship with God and therefore missed everything. Jesus made love and trust the focus of our relationship with God and ministered love and power everywhere He went. As the centurion understood, real submission requires trust in the one you submit to. We have been called to submit to God, but the foundation of submission is trust.

Most of us reading this would say that we love God and that we have committed our lives to Him. But do we trust Him? My son throws my granddaughter into the air and terrifies her mother in the process. My granddaughter knows her daddy loves her. She trusts him to catch her and howls with glee. Perhaps the crises in our individual lives are really nothing more than our Father God throwing us into the air to provide us an opportunity for fun and adventure as we discover and experience the thrill of being caught by Him.

I suggest that the only reason life's "adventures" fail to be fun is that we have not yet learned to trust the Father. Faith has not yet become the bridge connecting us to the experience of His love. The truth is that He catches us whether we trust Him or not. I have witnessed this reality over and over again, and yet so many of us continue to experience misery when we could be laughing. This was the lesson when Jesus stilled the storm as the disciples rowed for their lives. They sat miserable, sweaty, exhausted and afraid when they could have been laughing. It could have been an adventure instead of a nightmare.

In the summer of 2007 I took a team to minister in Ukraine through our church network in Eastern Europe. There I met Elena, a musician/songwriter who plays Ukraine's national instrument, the bandura, a kind of 66-string harp shaped like a guitar with a wide, round body and a short, fretless neck. Knowing that my church had a recording studio and that I am a fellow musician, she told the Lord that she would like to record her songs with me, since good recording facilities are hard to find in Ukraine. Laying a fleece before the Lord, she told Him that she would say nothing unless I offered. The first time I heard her play, the words came tumbling out of my mouth: "If you can get to the United States, I can make a professional recording for you."

Enormous obstacles stood before us. Many parts of Ukraine remain in poverty. Elena and her husband had no money. Hearts filled with love, the team I took with me assured Elena and her husband that we could raise the money to bring them to the United States, not knowing that recession would strike and that money would be in short supply. Worse, our State Department routinely refuses to grant visas to Ukrainians who wish to visit. Nevertheless, we set a date and began to pray. My heart sank as we were able to raise only five hundred dollars of the more than two thousand dollars Elena and Miroslav would need to fly here and I grieved as I composed an email apologizing to Elena for our failure.

Elena emailed back saying, "We're coming anyway." Long before their appointment with the American embassy they borrowed money from a friend and purchased their tickets, not knowing for certain whether they would even be permitted to come. I called it "crazy faith"! At the embassy they witnessed other Ukrainians with better reasons for coming being denied visas. One individual even promised to leave her small child in Ukraine in order to ensure her return! Denied! And yet our immigration officials granted Elena and her husband five-year visas!

There is more! When they arrived, I asked Elena to perform just two of her songs for our congregation on a Sunday morning. Our people responded with an offering in excess of one thousand five hundred dollars, covering the cost of the trip nearly in full. God calls us to adventures in Him, but we will never experience them apart from radical trust!

Recovering the Adventure

Somewhere along the way I lost the sense of adventure that I knew when I packed up my pregnant wife and left for seminary with nothing in my pocket but my faith and trust in the Father who provides for me. For many years thereafter I lived under the resultant cloud of fear and oppression, but the time came when I decided to take back what I had lost and to lead my people to do the same. Whether young or old, the greatest adventures of our lives lie ahead. I have been recovering the sense of adventure and fun I surrendered all those years ago. It should have been that way all along.

This kind of faith must form the heart of any prophetic statement we make to a needy world. The bulk of that message will be spoken through the example of our attitude and the atmosphere of hope that surrounds us as a people.

Increasing Faith

The Twelve had been with Jesus and had listened to His teaching concerning faith. Over and over again they had witnessed miracles connected with trust. I believe it had begun to dawn on them that they needed more of something they had too little of, and so they asked Him, "Increase our faith!" The Lord said, "If you had faith like a mustard seed, you would say to this mulberry tree, 'Be uprooted and be planted in the sea'; and it would obey you" (Luke 17:5–6).

Looking back once more to the story of the demon who refused to leave the boy in Matthew 17, we hear the disciples asking why they could not cast it out and Jesus replying in verse 20, "Because of the littleness of your faith; for truly I say to you, if you have faith the size of a mustard seed, you will say to this mountain, 'Move from here to there,' and it will move; and nothing will be impossible to you."

In these extreme statements concerning faith we encounter a challenge and a mystery. When Jesus desired to build their

153

trust and thereby increase their expectation of what God could do, He gave them neither a method to pursue, nor a set of confessions to recite. He unveiled neither verbal formulas nor any other means of speaking things into reality. In fact, because He knew that no amount of human striving could magnify faith by the smallest fraction of an ounce, He issued no instructions at all.

Paraphrased, Jesus told them, "If you really trusted God, you would have authority to command and all creation would obey you." Was this not Adam's birthright in the dominion given him over the earth before he fell into sin? And would this not be part of what Jesus now restores to us as we walk in the redemption He purchased for us with His death and resurrection? What Adam surrendered, Jesus recovers for us.

The mystery lies in the vision He set before them in answer to their request. Rather than give them instructions to follow by human effort, Jesus simply placed a bigger vision before them, as if to say, "Don't build your trust on past failures, like not being able to cast a demon out of a boy. Do you want to overcome your lack of faith? Adopt a bigger vision."

Accordingly, my church and I have been working at expanding our expectations of life as believers and of what we believe God to do. We work harder these days at celebrating the victories, healings and miracles of all kinds, no matter how small or large, because we know that in so doing we create an atmosphere of trust and expectation. We serve a God who is "able to do far more abundantly beyond all that we ask or think, according to the power that works within us" (Ephesians 3:20). Power flows more freely in a positive atmosphere that reinforces godly trust and expectation. How could a prophetic voice possibly rise from a people steeped in negativity, lacking an adequate grasp of the love, power and sovereignty of the God they represent?

The Principle of the Outrageous Prayer

Something happened to Beth and me in my last year of seminary, 1976, that I failed to understand at the time, although it makes sense now in light of the principle of the bigger vision Jesus set before the disciples. I had served two years part-time as the youth director in a good evangelical church affiliated with a liberal denomination when disaster struck. The gentle Bible-believing pastor I served under suffered a breakdown that forced him into retirement. To everyone's dismay, the denominational hierarchy sent in a liberal replacement who took offense at my Bible teaching and the manifestations of the Spirit the youth under my care were experiencing. Conflicting philosophies finally forced my resignation, which left my wife and me living entirely by faith without a regular income.

For the first and only time in our lives Beth and I fell behind on our bills and could not pay our rent. We cried out to God in desperation, protesting that we had always tithed and where was His promise of adequate provision? In the midst of all this, the Lord spoke to me clearly: *You've only asked Me to sustain you. I want you to honor My greatness by asking Me to make you rich.* I saw that we had become accustomed to living on the edge, to having just enough and no more. We had accepted this as normal, which might not have been a bad thing, except that living with that mindset failed to reflect the Lord's plan for us. He loves us much more than that.

Obediently, just to honor Him, I prayed that God would make us rich. In our mailbox the next day I found a stack of bills in ones and twenties wrapped in white paper—enough to pay the back rent, the rent for the current month and the Lord's tithe. I never learned who put it there.

Maybe I should call this "the principle of the outrageous prayer" flowing from faith expressed as trust in the greatness and love of Father God. At that particular point in my life as a penniless seminary student, I needed to honor the magnitude of His love by making an outrageous request. He assigned me an exercise in trusting His greatness and in refusing to settle for the kind of poverty that does Him no honor.

Faith and Authority

Jesus' authority in His earthly ministry flowed from perfect rest and trust in His Father. We can ask in faith obediently as I did in 1976, but Jesus offers us a higher level of trust that looks very much like that which He had in His Father. This results in authority to speak the word of command in His name. When we do so, creation obeys.

You see this in Peter when he met the lame beggar at the gate of the Temple shortly after the Holy Spirit filled the disciples with power on the Day of Pentecost. He did not *ask* God to heal the beggar. He rather spoke with authority to *command* the beggar to rise and walk.

> But Peter said, "I do not possess silver and gold, but what I do have I give to you: In the name of Jesus Christ the Nazarene—walk!" And seizing him by the right hand, he raised him up; and immediately his feet and his ankles were strengthened. With a leap he stood upright and began to walk; and he entered the temple with them, walking and leaping and praising God.
>
> Acts 3:6–8

After years of struggle on various fronts, many of us have settled for the status quo in the same way that my wife and I settled into a pattern of poverty and accepted it as normal back in our seminary days. This does no honor to our God. I suggest that we must begin to pray outrageous prayers for things as huge as telling a tree to move itself or asking the Lord to make us rich just to honor His love, power and desire for us. In order to do this, many of us must choose not to accept the loss of our dreams, those things God called us to long ago. Concerning our dreams and callings, we must begin to pray prayers of outsized expectation and intensity. When the doors begin to open as a result of that praying, we must be prepared to move forward in faith to take active risks.

Most of us need to get bigger visions for our churches and our lives and then honor God by boldly praying those visions. We must look for the day when our rest and trust in the Father run so deep that we move in His authority to command wonders and to finally fulfill the promise Jesus made in John 14:12: "Truly, truly, I say to you, he who believes in Me, the works that I do, he will do also; and greater works than these he will do; because I go to the Father."

PRAYER, PRAISE AND POWER

11

Praying as a Prophetic People

A prophetic people live and move in an atmosphere of faith. It follows that they must pray in a similar way, trusting God for all that He has declared and promised concerning us. When we pray on the basis of what we have already been given, we cease to pray prayers of anxiety and begin to pray declarative prophetic prayers. The following is a set of declarative prayers and affirmations that I led my congregation in by way of establishing these things firmly in our hearts as a part of our congregational mindset. They arise from faith, based on God's fulfilled promises, rather than from our own assessment of what we feel we do not have.

> I am chosen of God for a divine purpose on this earth.
> I have been filled with the Holy Spirit to easily and joyfully fulfill that destiny.
> I have received the Kingdom of God with all my brothers and sisters.

Heaven has come to earth in Jesus. Jesus dwells in
  me and among my brothers and sisters. I walk in
  heaven's glory.
We will therefore together demonstrate the Father's
  love to others.
Signs and wonders will follow after me because it is
  my birthright by the promise of God.
When I pray for the sick, they will be healed.
When I bless others, lives will be changed.
My heart will be love, my actions supernatural.
Amen.

Most of us need to learn to pray differently than we have
in the past, with a fresh approach, a new attitude and at a
greater depth that takes us farther into the presence of God
and into a greater place of victory than we have gone before.
We have received the Kingdom of God, heaven come to earth.
As a prophetic people, we must learn to live it at home, at
church, at work and in prayer.

Praying in Jesus' Name

Crucial to moving forward in declarative forms of prayer is a
clear understanding of what it means to pray in Jesus' name.
This will illuminate every teaching Jesus delivered concerning the Father's response to our prayers and will point us in
a direction of power and authority that I fear too few of us
have ever touched or experienced.

In Bible times, to act in the name of another meant that
you had been authorized to act as the sender for the sender
for a specific purpose. It was sometimes said that the man
sent by the man is the man himself. We might see it as a form
of power of attorney, but like our modern power of attorney,
the authority granted applies specifically to a defined set of
permissions. The power of prayer lies not in the words we
speak "in Jesus' name," like some magical power booster we

tack on to the end of a petition. Rather, it rests more in who we are at the moment of our prayer. It means that we approach the Father as if to say, "Father, Jesus sent me to make this request." "In Jesus' name" means that we represent Jesus and that our prayer flows from intimacy and oneness with Him in which we have discerned and sensed His will in some way so that we know that we have permission to make our request.

I recall as a child asking my father if I could go to the movies. He would answer, "What did your mother say?" I knew the drill. I had already been to her and could therefore answer with authority, "She said I could go." On that basis Dad would agree. Once in a long while I told my father that I had my mother's permission when I did not, but for a week after such an attempt at deception, the shape of my world took a radically different form. I got the message!

Similarly, praying in Jesus' name means that I go before the Father saying in effect, "Father, Jesus said I could ask this. I'm representing Him." To pray in Jesus' name therefore requires that we learn to represent Jesus accurately, to be in oneness with Him as we approach the Father.

Toward that end we have been filled with the Holy Spirit, the Spirit of Jesus. When He came to dwell in us, He brought with Him His mind, the mind of Christ. In 1 Corinthians 2:16, in the context of writing about what it means to be spiritual men and women, the apostle Paul clearly stated that we have the mind of Christ. We therefore have this as a present possession, not reserved for some time in the future when we at last become whole or holy enough. We have His mind in the here and now. We might not yet be in agreement with it, we might even be caught in a kind of struggle for dominance between His mind and ours, and we might not yet fully believe the truth of what we have been given, but it remains resident in us for us to discover.

Therefore, when we pray—and if we pray with the mind of Christ that we have already been given—then we state the will of Jesus, representing Him before Father God. As we accurately represent Jesus, Father God always responds because He never ignores His Son. Keep this in mind as we take a look at some of the extreme statements Jesus made concerning prayer.

Words of Command and Believing to Receive

Undoubtedly catching the disciples' attention, Jesus said,

> "Truly I say to you, whoever says to this mountain, 'Be taken up and cast into the sea,' and does not doubt in his heart, but believes that what he says is going to happen, it will be granted him. Therefore I say to you, all things for which you pray and ask, believe *that you have received them*, and they will be granted you."
>
> Mark 11:23–24, emphasis mine

Would it not be lots of fun if these verses really did mean something like this: "I want a top-of-the-line Lexus to drive, Lord. Now I believe that I have received that Lexus"? And behold! There it is behind door number three! We all know this will not happen any time soon and we easily recognize it as silliness. No matter how hard I might seek to believe that a new Lexus will be waiting in my driveway in the morning, I will nevertheless find my humble bottom-of-the-line Mitsubishi Lancer gazing affectionately back at me. Beyond silliness, we ought to recognize this kind of thing as a travesty of faith born of self-centered greed.

I also think it rather silly to work at confessing that we have already received a healing that has not yet manifested physically in a measurable way. Some of us have been taught to do this, but in 32 years of full-time ministry I have never seen it work, because this is not what Jesus meant. I am not claiming that it has never happened—only that in the hundreds of cases I have witnessed over the years, I have not personally seen it work. I strongly suspect that in cases where people have claimed it worked, the cause was more the incredible mercy of God than the validity of the method.

In reality, we are healed when we are healed. Never did Jesus tell anyone to confess a healing that had not yet manifested in the natural. We have a wheelchair-bound paraplegic in our church. Would it not be ridiculous for her to proclaim, "I know I've been healed; I have received my ability to walk!" while she remains bound to her wheelchair? We want to be a prophetic people impacting the community around us. What kind of message would such an approach send to outsiders? Would they not dismissively mutter, "Those people are out of their minds!"?

For the record, as we have prayed for our paraplegic over a number of months, she has begun to experience sensations in her legs for the first time in her life. On a few occasions she has been able to generate some small movement. We will not declare her complete healing until her healing is complete, but we will thank God for what has been accomplished and take her current progress as both a call to pray and a promise of what is yet to come.

The Truth of It

The cultural context of a biblical statement has as much to do with the actual meaning of a passage of Scripture as the literal definitions of the words themselves. From culture to culture and age to age, language usage and figures of speech change. If, therefore, we fail to understand certain figures of speech in the context of the culture in which they were spoken, then we will inevitably misunderstand the true message.

For instance, today when one of our American young people wants to say that something is really wonderful, he or she exclaims, "That's sick!" Imagine someone reading such an exclamation two thousand years later with no understanding of the cultural context in which it was spoken! What kind of conclusion might he draw? Would he not mistakenly think the speaker meant, "That's diseased!"?

In the context of first-century Jewish culture in Palestine, when a teacher wanted to drive home a significantly important point and make it really stick, he employed a linguistic device called "Hebrew hyperbole." He might express his point in such an extreme form that it would seem to be impossible or even illogical, never meaning it to be taken literally—only intensely.

When I was a child my mother employed a similar technique when she told me that if I did not stop whatever trouble I was getting into she would spank me until I could not sit down for a week. I knew that would never happen, but I also knew for certain that she was about to have a "conniption fit" and that I had better get out of her way. The use of hyperbole made her meaning both powerful and memorable.

In a similar way Jesus spoke in Hebrew hyperbole when He declared in Luke 14:26, "If anyone comes to Me, and does not hate his own father and mother and wife and children and brothers and sisters, yes, and even his own life, he cannot be My disciple." Obviously He did not really intend that we should hate, especially not when in other passages He exhorted us to love, care for and respect our parents. He simply used a hyperbolic figure of speech to drive home the crucial point that those who would be His disciples must love Him intensely above all else. Statements concerning moving mountains and believing that we have already received anything we have asked for similarly reflect a measure of Hebrew hyperbole that points us toward strong trust in the Lord.

Prayers of Unbelief versus Prayers of Faith

Clearly, Jesus wanted us to understand that we must pray on the basis of what we have already received from God rather than praying prayers of unbelief based on our perceptions of lack. For instance, at this writing the Lord has told me—at least for the time being—not to ask for revival in my church with all of its manifestations in life changes, healing, worship, victory out there in world and all the rest. Why? Because this would be a prayer of unbelief, not of faith. He has already sent us revival and given us evidence of it, although we do not yet see the fullness of what we would like to see. It is therefore time to start walking in what we have already been given instead of living in denial of it, blind to what He is already doing.

How do I know that we have already been given revival? Hear Jesus' promise: "If you then, being evil, know how to give good gifts to your children, how much more will your heavenly Father give the Holy Spirit to those who ask Him?" (Luke 11:13). I know that I have asked and that our Father keeps His Word. I see evidence of revival in the spiritual gifts, proven healings and life changes I witness in my people every day. On that basis, I should rather be praying in a declarative manner, *You have filled me with Your Holy Spirit and shown me the evidence. I receive You. Thank You for revival.* In this case I am not confessing in a vacuum. I am declaring in faith what God has both promised in His Word and already demonstrated in measurable terms.

Recall Acts 2:38–39: "Peter said to them, 'Repent, and each of you be baptized in the name of Jesus Christ for the forgiveness of your sins; and you will receive the gift of the Holy Spirit. For the promise is for you and your children and for all who are far off, as many as the Lord our God will call to Himself.'" I know that I have repented and been baptized. On the basis of this promise, I have therefore already been forgiven and have already been filled with the Spirit just as the disciples were filled on the Day of Pentecost when they first spoke with other tongues and then won three thousand to Jesus. I, too, have experienced His touch and, like the disciples, I speak in tongues. On that basis, I know that everything they could do, I can do. I have received what they received. My declarative prayer will therefore be, "Lord, I can do all things through Your Spirit who fills me." I will pray on the basis of what I have already been given.

Of course, this does not take into account matters of degree and scope. While I know what I have been given, I am aware that we have not yet experienced in reality anything like the great revivals of the past: the First Great Awakening in the early to mid-1700s, the Second Great Awakening in the first decade of the 1800s, Azusa Street in 1906. What God has placed in my heart has not yet exploded to impact the nations. For degree and scope I will therefore continue to pray, but in faith I will rest in the revival I have already been granted.

Why do I ask for the gift of healing as if it were not already given to me? Why pray that prayer of unbelief? Jesus told us to believe that we have already received that for which we have asked, based on what He has told us we have already been given. This does not come without evidence. Healings happen on a regular basis in my church and ministry. Mark 16:17–18 teaches, "These signs will accompany those who have believed: in My name they will cast out demons, they will speak with new tongues; they will pick up serpents, and if they drink any deadly poison, it will not hurt them; they will lay hands on the sick, and they will recover." For those who have not yet seen this evidence, Jesus calls you to begin taking the "risk." Pray for others. Act on the basis of what He has declared concerning you. You and I can pray for the sick, not in unbelief as if asking for something we do not yet have, but in faith on the basis of what Jesus says we already possess and has already given evidence of.

I can believe that I have already received what He has told me I already have.

Declarative Prayers

On the basis of what we have already received, we must learn to pray declarative prayers, speaking to the Father what is true. "Lord, You have given me Your Spirit. You have touched me, changed me and provided for me. You have chosen me and loved me. You have made me holy. Your gifts dwell in me. You are doing great things in my life and in my church."

For those who require a scriptural model for declarative prayer, hear the words of Jesus in Matthew 11:25–26: "At that time Jesus said, 'I praise You, Father, Lord of heaven and earth, that You have hidden these things from the wise and intelligent and have revealed them to infants. Yes, Father, for this way was well-pleasing in Your sight.'" In this case Jesus declared what the Father had already accomplished rather than request that it be done.

A more dramatic example can be found in John 11:41–42. Jesus' friend Lazarus had been dead four days when Jesus arrived and commanded them to remove the stone from the entrance to the tomb. It reads, "So they removed the stone. Then Jesus raised His eyes, and said, 'Father, I thank You that You have heard Me. I knew that You always hear Me; but because of the people standing around I said it, so that they may believe that You sent Me.'" As He stood before the tomb of His friend, Jesus prayed a declarative prayer out loud, not just so that the Father would hear, but to strengthen the certainty, hope and faith of those who had gathered to witness His actions. The result? "When He had said these things, He cried out with a loud voice, 'Lazarus, come forth.' The man who had died came forth, bound hand and foot with wrappings, and his face was wrapped around with a cloth. Jesus said to them, 'Unbind him, and let him go'" (11:43–44).

Jesus did not beg the Father to raise Lazarus. He rather declared what He had received and what He knew He had already been given. In the process He built up the people around Him in faith and then acted to issue a command and perform a miracle.

Too often we pray like paupers who have nothing. In so doing we erode what ought to be an atmosphere of faith and encouragement. We then fail to notice when He sends the things we requested because the atmosphere of unbelief we have created and reinforced with our style of praying blinds us to it. We pray on the basis of our fear and anxiety rather than from the certainty of what we have already been given.

In declarative prayer we build an atmosphere of hope that lifts people into the presence of God, and we cultivate a culture of faith and trust in God who never fails. Ultimately we do this not for ourselves but for a world desperate for hope and filled with people who need to know that God is real. When we pray from a basis in our anxiety we actually feed an atmosphere of negativity that drags us down and everyone else with us. We must therefore learn to pray differently. By making such extreme statements using Hebrew hyperbole, Jesus led us to pray in hope and in harmony with His Spirit, based on what God has already given us in His Kingdom and in His love. He spoke of great things happening in our lives through our prayers. He taught of favor from heaven for every aspect of life from the heart of a Father who loves us more than we can understand.

The Prayer of Agreement

Again I say to you, that if two of you agree on earth about anything that they may ask, it shall be done for them by My Father who is in heaven. For where two or three have gathered together in My name, I am there in their midst.

Matthew 18:19–20

We examined one aspect of the prayer of agreement in chapter two. In this context, remember the qualifier: When we pray "in Jesus' name," representing Him, we pray what He has told us to pray. Therefore, agreement must not be viewed as a form of ganging up on God to get Him to do whatever we want Him to do. God does not hold referendums. He does not listen to the advice of focus groups. He has no advisors and takes no votes.

The principle of agreement means that we seek Him together, enter His presence together and hear from Him together so that we agree together concerning His voice. We achieve a unified sense of His guidance for prayer, and we lift our voices in unity based on the guidance we have heard.

For example, the church I pastor has undergone a major change of spirit and attitude over the last couple of years. We moved from a heart of contention, suspicion and criticism to a heart of love, unity, honor and blessing. I have long been convinced that in most cases we must first accomplish in prayer what we hope to experience in reality. Accordingly, the shift in our congregation began as we sought God together in our intercessory meetings. Together we came into agreement concerning what we believed God wanted us to become. Then, in a spirit of oneness, we cried to God to bring it about.

Two things resulted. First, in our oneness with one another God saw an essential element of His own nature reflected back to Him. Second, in discerning together the will of our Savior and agreeing together concerning what we had heard, we could then approach the Father "in Jesus' name," truly representing Him. When God sees these two things, He responds.

Receiving All Things You Ask

> And Jesus answered and said to them, "Truly I say to you, if you have faith and do not doubt, you will not only do what was done to the fig tree, but even if you say to this mountain, 'Be taken up and cast into the sea,' it will happen. And all things you ask in prayer, believing, you will receive."
>
> Matthew 21:21–22

The key to the word *all* lies in the act of believing, but in this context what does it mean to believe? Should we view belief as some kind of mysterious state of mental certainty? Or ought we rather to understand what it means to trust the Father? Should we rather plumb the depths of oneness with Him? When we grow in oneness with Him and then speak to creation as one with the Father, the world moves. Creation obeys not because we have achieved some mysterious power called faith, but because our faith, our trust, rests in the Father to such an extent that the Holy Spirit moves freely through us to affect the world around us.

Jesus Himself performed mighty miracles, but He made it abundantly clear that He never acted on His own. He did only what He saw His Father doing and said only what He heard His Father saying. His authority flowed from faith and trust, a surrendered will and oneness with His Father. Because His words reflected the will of the Father, creation obeyed.

Accordingly, when our words reflect the will of Jesus and flow from oneness with Him, creation obeys. This constitutes the faith element. If we had faith like that when we needed to move mountains, we would boldly issue the command and creation would obey.

Conclusion

Praying as a prophetic people includes three basic elements, two of which we have already examined. First, we engage in *declarative prayer*, stating what already exists and what we have already been given by the Father's Word. We thereby build an atmosphere of faith and hope. Second, we *pray in agreement*, which we understand to be unified discernment of His will as we seek Him together with other believers.

Finally we *pray with perseverance.* I saved this for last because I understand the difficulty involved. Perseverance requires that we grow, labor and often stretch ourselves in sacrifice.

Now He was telling them a parable to show that at all times they ought to pray and not to lose heart, saying, "In a certain city there was a judge who did not fear God and did not respect man. There was a widow in that city, and she kept coming to him, saying, 'Give me legal protection from my opponent.' For a while he was unwilling; but afterward he said to himself, 'Even though I do not fear God nor respect man, yet because this widow bothers me, I will give her legal protection, otherwise by continually coming she will wear me out.'" And the Lord said, "Hear what the unrighteous judge said; now, will not God bring about justice for His elect who cry to Him day and night, and will He delay long over them? I tell you that He will bring about justice for them quickly. However, when the Son of Man comes, will He find faith on the earth?"

Luke 18:1–8

As a child there were times when I asked for things and my parents granted them freely and easily, but more often they made me work for what I desired. I recall asking, "Dad, can I have a BB gun?" He replied, "If you can earn the money you can have anything, son." He knew that I needed to grow up and that I would never grow up if everything came easily. Likewise, our heavenly Father often calls us to grow up and therefore requires us to sacrifice for things.

Personally, for more than fourteen years I prayed for my current congregation to become what it is now growing into. If it had come easily I would never have learned the wisdom I have garnered from having to work for it. If I had given up and stopped praying, we would still be back there walking through the mud and ugliness instead of watching the glory expand.

I have exhorted my people not to give up praying for the husband or wife, their children or parents who might seem so far from God and so deeply mired in trouble. God honors sacrifice. Often the sacrifice required is your own perseverance.

Some forms of healing require a similar sacrifice of labor in prayer offered over extended periods of time. In the church I served in Idaho during the 1980s we began to pray for a young man with a severe hearing impairment. At first he noticed little or no difference, but subsequent testing revealed a 10 percent improvement. We continued to pray. A month or two later a second test measured another 10 percent improvement. This continued over a period of about a year until his hearing tested nearly normal.

We therefore persevere as we pray declarative prayers, remembering what we have been given while we seek the heart of Jesus in order to represent Him accurately before the Father.

12

A Prophetic Atmosphere of Praise

If God anoints declarative prayers, then we certainly must learn to declare our praise as we engage in worship! In the context of a book on becoming a prophetic people, one might expect a discussion of praise and worship to be focused on elements like musical forms, prophetic songs and forms of prophetic dance. Much has been written on such subjects, some of it by me. However, my focus here is not on our outward forms of worship, but rather on the creation of an atmosphere of hope, expectation, faith and power in the local church that contributes to a prophetic impact on the community. These elements of atmosphere comprise the substance that must fill whatever forms we employ. Apart from these elements of substance, outward forms amount to little more than empty noise, while, by contrast, prophetic anointing takes us somewhere and accomplishes the purposes of the Lord. This chapter addresses foundational issues of praise and worship for creating a substantive atmosphere that realizes these purposes. I leave the forms and applications to the individual congregation.

Praise as a Strategy

In that light, 1 Chronicles 25:1 contains a curious note. As King David neared the end of his life, he began to set the stage for his son to succeed him, gathering materials for the Temple to be built under Solomon and setting the military commanders and the army in order. "Moreover, David and the commanders of the army set apart for the service some of the sons of Asaph and of Heman and of Jeduthun, who were to prophesy with lyres, harps and cymbals."

The commanders of the *army* set up the prophetic worshipers? Why not the priests? Why not the elders of Israel? I believe David's officers understood something we often miss. David and his generals understood strategy on the battlefield. Especially when facing larger and better-equipped forces, they knew the need for advantage and how to gain it.

Therefore, as they prepared for Solomon's succession to the throne, they established worship as a force multiplier to strengthen the army for the defense of their nation. They thought of effective worship as a source of military advantage not merely to be offered up at times of perceived need, but to be established as a daily and continual flow in the Temple of the Lord. To be of military value, it had to be consistent.

David built his entire life around praise and worship, from the times he spent as a boy alone in the field caring for his father's sheep, to the days of his maturity as the leader of the people of God. For this reason, where worship is concerned, he stands as the most towering figure of the Old Testament. It can be no accident that he steeped himself in worship and at the same time reigned as a victorious warrior king. The connection cannot be missed.

Although I reject the all too commonly held belief that prophetic people must of necessity become warriors, I do accept the fact that the whole Body of Christ is engaged in spiritual warfare and will be so engaged until Jesus returns. The Bible contains ample evidence that prophetic people often played

176

key roles in warfare. As a prophetic people we have been called to be involved in a continuing struggle "against the rulers, against the powers, against the world forces of this darkness, against the spiritual forces of wickedness in the heavenly places" (Ephesians 6:12). To be victorious in this on-going conflict, we must be a worshiping people at heart. Just as David and his military commanders established worship as a strategic military necessity, so we as a prophetic people must establish our own power base in worship in order to prophetically affect change in the world around us. Some key elements for establishing that power base follow.

Remembering the Works of the Lord

Psalm 111 declares, "Praise the LORD! I will give thanks to the LORD with all my heart, in the company of the upright and in the assembly. Great are the works of the LORD; they are studied by all who delight in them" (verses 1–2). In an established lifestyle of worship we must diligently examine the works of the Lord and determine to remember them. We must celebrate them, draw lessons from them and make them part of our individual and corporate lives.

As an individual, have you ever been rescued by God? How many times has He done this? For example, one family in the church I pastor fell on difficult economic times when the plant closed at which the breadwinner worked. As unemployment impacted them, they fell behind financially and faced the possible loss of their home. Just in time, God came through with a very lucrative job that paid the bills and caught them up. A couple of years later, that same scenario repeated itself, but they remembered the previous rescue and drew strength from it to face the new crisis. We must do more than remember what God did in Bible times. We must hold on to what He has done in our personal past. What He did yesterday, He will do again. He is the same yesterday, today and forever.

In 2006, my garage door died and the sump pump quit all in one month. The total economic blow added up to about twelve thousand dollars that we did not have at the time, but just a week later I received a royalty check from my publisher that covered the entire expense. Should I moan, groan, complain and be depressed that every time extra money comes in and we try to get ahead, some disaster takes it away, or should I praise the goodness of God that He provided what we needed when we needed it? And should I not remember that He has done this for us consistently and faithfully over the years? If I can praise God in this way, remembering His great works and celebrating them, then I will lead a joyous and power-filled life. If I cannot, I will remain weak and depressed with nothing of value to say to a needy world.

We will never be a truly prophetic people until we learn to remember and celebrate what God has done, even under the worst of circumstances. I say again that what God has done in the past, He will do again. Prophetic impact in the present will therefore be rooted in remembrance of the past.

Speaking Aloud the Deeds of the Lord

"Oh give thanks to the LORD, call upon His name; make known His deeds among the peoples. Sing to Him, sing praises to Him; speak of all His wonders" (Psalm 105:1–2). God's people diminish themselves when they choose not to speak of the deeds of the Lord, and choose rather to speak of obstacles and negatives. We must choose to be vocal concerning what God is doing and has done. This includes the healings we have seen, the times we have been rescued by Him, the homes He has provided for us and all the occasions on which He has restored our broken hearts.

"Glory in His holy name; let the heart of those who seek the LORD be glad. Seek the LORD and His strength; seek His face continually. Remember His wonders which He has done, His marvels and the judgments uttered by His mouth" (Psalm 105:3–5). Notice the connection between strength and rehearsing the deeds of God in praise (see verses 1–5). This kind of praise forms a prophetic force multiplier that renders us more powerful than the obstacles we face.

As Paul and Silas preached in Philippi they came upon a slave girl with a demon of divination who made a lot of money for her owners by telling fortunes. Irritated with her loud and distracting proclamations of the identity of Paul and Silas, Paul cast the spirit out of her and ended the profit-making venture. Angered, her owners spread lies and slander against Paul and Silas, which resulted in a trial before the authorities who then had them severely beaten with rods and locked in the stocks in the inner prison.

> But about midnight Paul and Silas were praying and sing-ing hymns of praise to God, and the prisoners were listen-ing to them; and suddenly there came a great earthquake, so that the foundations of the prison house were shaken; and immediately all the doors were opened and everyone's chains were unfastened. When the jailer awoke and saw the prison doors opened, he drew his sword and was about to kill himself, supposing that the prisoners had escaped. But Paul cried out with a loud voice, saying, "Do not harm yourself, for we are all here!" And he called for lights and rushed in, and trembling with fear he fell down before Paul and Silas, and after he brought them out, he said, "Sirs, what must I do to be saved?"
>
> Acts 16:25–30

The jailer received Jesus and then took them to his home; under Paul's preaching his entire household was saved and filled with the Spirit.

Could Paul and Silas have felt sorry for themselves over their painful misfortune? Of course. Would they have had a right to? Certainly. I personally experience tremendous dif-ficulty working through pain, whether physical or emotional, but that night Paul and Silas made an important decision concerning how they would respond to suffering and where they would focus their attention. Circumstances made that decision exceedingly difficult, but they persevered and offered up a vocal sacrifice in worship that the whole prison could hear.

In that miserable place and in the midst of their suffering, worship focused their attention on God's goodness and power. This rendered them more powerful than the situation they faced and loosed the power of God to overcome overwhelming obstacles. Ministry—a prophetic impact—resulted that brought a whole household into the Kingdom of God.

Cataloging the Negatives

In 1 Samuel 13 King Saul faced an overwhelming enemy. Apparently, he had just 3,000 men at his disposal, against the Philistines' "30,000 chariots and 6,000 horsemen, and people like the sand which is on the seashore in abundance" (verse 5). The prophet Samuel instructed him to wait seven days for him to return to offer sacrifice and seek the Lord's favor. Seven days for that small army to stare fear in the face! Samuel delayed, and as fear took ever deeper root in their hearts, Saul's army began to scatter. In an effort to hold his men together and secure the Lord's favor, Saul offered the sacrifice himself in presumptuous disobedience to the Lord's command through Samuel.

> As soon as he finished offering the burnt offering, behold, Samuel came; and Saul went out to meet him and to greet him. But Samuel said, "What have you done?" And Saul said, "Because I saw that the people were scattering from me, and that you did not come within the appointed days, and that the Philistines were assembling at Michmash, therefore I said, 'Now the Philistines will come down against me at Gilgal, and

I have not asked the favor of the LORD.' So I forced myself and offered the burnt offering."

verses 10–12

In response to Saul's foolish disobedience, Samuel revoked his anointing as king and ended his dynasty before it could begin, but Saul's losses stemmed from a deeper cause than mere disobedience. Rather than lead a life of disciplined worship, Saul became one who cataloged negatives. Israel needed a king after God's own heart, a man of worship, someone who would remember and rehearse the nature and the deeds of God in the face of every obstacle. Such a lifestyle facilitates obedience while negativity inevitably leads to violation. David, the worshiper, therefore replaced Saul, the cataloger of negatives.

If praise stands out as a force multiplier, then it would be reasonable to assume that some things can function as force minimizers. As I have already noted, Saul apparently could not or would not stop cataloging the negatives. He forgot—or chose not to remember—all that God had done for him and his people in the past. Thus blinded to the true nature of the assets at his disposal, he failed to wait for and act upon the power of heaven.

Once we begin to dwell on the negatives, we precipitate a downward spiral into ever deeper fear and depression. Once this has been sown into a local Body of Christ and becomes part of the atmosphere or spirit of the fellowship, we inevitably fail to do what God has called us to do. We find ourselves weakened and unable to prevail when the battle comes to us—or even when the promise of God arrives. Saul therefore forfeited both his anointing as king and the right to father a dynasty. Failure as a worshiper cost him his destiny. God therefore took what would have been Saul's posterity and transferred it to the man after His own heart—David, the worshiper.

Unfortunately, when setbacks or disappointments present themselves, too many of us, like Saul, begin to dwell on the negatives, rather than remember what God has done and all that He has established in our lives. This feeds and amplifies fear and depression, distorts perceptions, leads us to believe things that are not true and ultimately results in disobedience and destruction. Saul's undoing, the thing that weakened him and finally cost him his destiny, was that he chose to focus on his fears and then act on them.

This same dynamic led to Elijah's downfall in 1 Kings 18. Instead of remembering what God had just done through him in defeating the 450 prophets of Baal, he chose to dwell upon the negative when Jezebel threatened his life. In so doing, he fell from the kind of faith that called fire from heaven and defeated 450 prophets of Baal to such a state of weakness that he could not find it in himself to face down a verbal threat from just one woman. Instead, he fled to the wilderness where he whimpered and whined in depression and discouragement. As a result, the Lord told him to go home and appoint his successor, Elisha, someone younger and more filled with faith than he had chosen to be.

If praising God serves as a force multiplier, then the opposite, a focus on the negative, on grumbling and complaining, diminishes both you and your people to the point of powerlessness. Such a focus creates an atmosphere of negative expectation in the Body of Christ that chokes off the flow of significant prophetic impact.

Defeating Your Goliath

There will always be a negative on which to meditate somewhere in your life or fellowship. You will find it in your job. It will flow from the people around you for the simple reason that all of them are sinners. You will find plenty of negatives at home. How many of us know that the one we married will never meet our needs? Or that our children are not always the delight we bargained for when we first planned to have them? No matter what church you choose to attend, you will see it in the people who attend there, and it will surface in your judgments of the way things are done. You can meditate on those deficits, but if that is what you choose, then deficit and disappointment will become your whole world and you will be stripped of power by it.

How did David defeat Goliath? David could not have been more than fourteen years old, small in stature and perhaps a bit soft in appearance when he came to the battle as a runner to deliver provisions for his older brothers. First Samuel 17:4 tells us that Goliath stood as tall as six cubits and a span. Nearly ten feet! And he had covered himself with heavy armor and weaponry. Daily, he strode forth from the ranks of the Philistines and called for a man to fight with him. Daily, Israel fled in fear.

King Saul, the cataloger of negatives, reacted predictably. "When Saul and all Israel heard these words of the Philistine, they were dismayed and greatly afraid" (1 Samuel 17:11). Verse 24 continues, "When all the men of Israel saw the man, they fled from him and were greatly afraid." Saul and the whole army began adding up the negatives, forgetting everything God had ever done for them. Dread of the giant and of the Philistine army spread through the ranks like a contagious disease until the atmosphere of fear and unbelief they created stripped them of power. By the time David arrived they could do nothing but stand around trembling and wondering what to do.

David had never been to war and had never fought with or killed a man, much less a giant. He had only kept the wild animals away from his father's sheep while he waited for hair to grow in places where a man grows hair.

Uninfected by the atmosphere of fear and dismay that had so paralyzed Saul's army, young David boldly volunteered to fight Goliath. "Then Saul said to David, 'You are not able to go against this Philistine to fight with him; for you are but a youth while he has been a warrior from his youth'" (1 Samuel 17:33).

While Saul could only catalog the negatives and rehearse the impossibilities, David instinctively and deliberately remembered what God had done for him in the past and applied it to the current situation. First Samuel 17:34–37 says,

> But David said to Saul, "Your servant was tending his father's sheep. When a lion or a bear came and took a lamb from the flock, I went out after him and attacked him, and rescued it from his mouth; and when he rose up against me, I seized him by his beard and struck him and killed him. Your servant has killed both the lion and the bear; and this uncircumcised Philistine will be like one of them, since he has taunted the armies of the living God." And David said, "The LORD who delivered me from the paw of the lion and from the paw of the bear, He will deliver me from the hand of this Philistine." And Saul said to David, "Go, and may the LORD be with you."

The force multiplier of a worshipful life begins with remembering! David used his memories of the Lord's past deeds in his own life as the basis for facing an overwhelming and impossible obstacle in the present. He slew the giant with a single sling stone and then cut off Goliath's head with his own sword. David's courage and the power of his victory spread throughout the army of Israel, and the people of God won the battle that day. Prophetic impact by a prophetic lighthouse people requires an atmosphere of praise in which to thrive.

In 2 Samuel 22 David offered a lengthy song of praise to God, listing all the things God had done for him, but notice these two verses: "For You are my lamp, O LORD; and the LORD illumines my darkness. For by You I can run upon a troop; by my God I can leap over a wall" (verses 29–30). Praise enables one man alone to run through a troop of many, and to jump a city wall many times his own height.

Force multipliers like praise enable us to overcome obstacles, problems and situations that would overwhelm ordinary people; but we are not ordinary people. We are royalty, seated with Jesus in the heavenly places at the right hand of God and set to inherit with Him all that our royal Father owns and holds. Praise becomes such a people. It magnifies power and effectiveness for us, but it begins with a discipline and a choice.

At Last, the Decision

For the sake of personal testimony, I wish I could say that I have been consistent at praising God all my life. I know that I have been good at it when standing on a stage with a guitar in my hands and a microphone in my face as the anointing flows down from heaven for a congregation. I cannot, however, make such a claim concerning what happens when I am not on that stage and I must deal with everyday issues.

I have decided, however, that I will not live the remainder of my life that way. For my own sake, for the sake of my family and for the sake of the people I lead, I have made a firm decision. I will remember the works of the Lord, I will praise Him for them and there will be no obstacle to oppose the good purposes of God through me or through my people. Together we will work at creating an atmosphere of praise in which we remember and celebrate the deeds of the Lord, and we will therefore prophetically impact our world as we have been destined to do.

13

The Holy Spirit:
Vision, Power and Effect

Several chapters of this book have included "force multipliers." Let's review the definition: *A force multiplier is a factor that, when added, dramatically increases (hence "multiplies") the combat effectiveness of a military force.*

Example: A soldier hunts an enemy at night in the forest. Outnumbered ten to one, our soldier nevertheless has an advantage. With his pair of night vision goggles he can see in the dark where his enemies cannot. Those night vision goggles constitute the force multiplier that renders him more powerful than the enemy arrayed against him. The force multiplier enables him to overcome obstacles that would be overwhelming under any other circumstances.

The most powerful force multiplier available to any Christian or body of believers is the Person of the Holy Spirit indwelling us, none other than the Spirit of Jesus Himself who takes up residence in the heart of every sinner who repents and comes to Him. More than any other element or principle of force multiplication, He enables any local body of believers to achieve a prophetic impact. He infuses the honor we give one another, enables our oneness, puts fire in our praise, imparts prophetic words, teaches us servanthood and so much more.

The gift of the Spirit comes in three parts: vision, power and effect. Vision is *why* God sends the Holy Spirit. Power is the *ability* to do things that would be impossible without the Holy Spirit. The effect is *what happens* when the power moves through us.

The Vision

Three-Generational

God intended for us to pass the gift of the Holy Spirit as an inheritance to those who come after us. Peter included this three-generational vision in his sermon on the Day of Pentecost when he said in Acts 2:38–39 (emphasis mine),

> Repent, and each of you be baptized in the name of Jesus Christ for the forgiveness of your sins; and you will receive the gift of the Holy Spirit. For the promise is *for you and your children and for all who are far off*, as many as the Lord our God will call to Himself.

Two principles of inheritance flow from these verses. First, God promised the experience and exercise of the power of the Holy Spirit for everyone who believes, not just a special few, and not by measure. The gift is the whole gift, not merely a portion. Many years ago I heard a black woman preacher, "Rev Ev" Carter, challenge an audience with this question: "When the Holy Spirit came in, did He come in part of the way or all of the way?" The inescapable logic of her query stuck with me and has since shaped much of my theology of the Holy Spirit and His gifts.

188

In short, I may be a pastor and a leader, but I have no more of Him than any average believer who has received Jesus. He gave His whole self, not just a part or portion, to each one of us. In this gift, no member of the Body of Christ enjoys any more favor than any other member. Infinite love is like that. Everyone gets 100 percent of Daddy. When He chose to indwell you and me, He brought all His gifts with Him to fully equip every one of us for every good work.

It seems, however, that many of us persist in placing all the weight and anointing on the few whom we regard as gifted, while we allow our own gifts of the Spirit to lie dormant. We do this because we fail to truly believe that we ourselves have those gifts, or because we think someone else has more of the Holy Spirit than we do. Consequently, we have created a star system in the Body of Christ that exalts individuals instead of fostering a prophetic *people*—lighthouse churches changing their communities as a people together.

The truth is that God did give some of us as leaders. God created some of us for the platform and for equipping and deploying believers into ministry (see Ephesians 4:11) while He made others of us for less-visible service. In either case, He gave us each the same Holy Spirit in the same measure to fully equip and empower us for the ministries He called us to pursue.

Unfortunately, having been schooled in the star system, too many leaders have reserved the real power ministry for themselves and have therefore unwittingly cheated the Body of Christ of its birthright. Thus they lose sight of God's true three-generational vision for the gift.

The second idea Peter set forth as vision for the gift of the Spirit flows from the first. We must pass the gift of the Holy Spirit to our children, and to their children, and then to those who become our spiritual children by coming to know Jesus through us. Too many Christians in our time, both leadership and laity, have held only a one-generational vision for the gift of the Holy Spirit, if we had a vision for moving in

189

the power of the Spirit at all. We have treated the gift of the Spirit as if that gift were all about nothing more than meeting our personal needs and fostering our own self-fulfillment. As a result, the inheritance has stopped with us instead of multiplying in power through each new generation of believers. Historically, therefore, it has been the rare revival that lasted beyond the generation through which it came. God has a better plan, but we have somehow missed it!

This principle of generational increase explains why Elijah had a powerful anointing from the Spirit, but passed a double portion of what God had given him to his spiritual son, Elisha. Because of generational increase, made possible by the care and nurture Elijah gave him, Elisha performed greater miracles than did Elijah.

God's three-generational vision of increase explains why King David was said to be a man after God's own heart, but his son Solomon became the wisest man who had ever lived. Solomon led Israel to the pinnacle of its glory. Anointing, passed on by inheritance, increased in the next generation. It also explains why Jesus could promise in John 14:12 that we who believe would do the works that He did and greater works than He did. I believe He spoke from His Father's vision for the anointing of the Spirit, not only that it would be three-generational, but that it should increase in each successive generation.

This holds true for families, relationships and personal lives, as well as for ministry. My parents received the power of the Holy Spirit for the first time in 1958, when I was seven years old. In the years that followed, they gave my siblings and me a solid faith, schooled us in the things of the Spirit and gave us an experience of Him. Nevertheless, two of their six children suffered disastrous marital lives, and all six of us have had to work through significant issues of inner healing.

However, because of what I inherited from them in the Holy Spirit, I have passed a third-generational increase of anointing to my own children. They have become better parents than my wife and I were. Their inheritance resonates in the health of their marriages and in the power of their service to the Lord. Their fruit far exceeds that which their mother and I produced when we were their age.

Already I see them passing the increase of Holy Spirit anointing to their own children. Even at just nine months old, for example, my grandson, Gabriel, has ministered to others in power. In the checkout line at the supermarket the child in the stroller next to him began screaming inconsolably. Gabriel fixed his gaze on her and stretched out his hand. Immediately, the crying stopped and the child began to laugh. Not infrequently he lovingly lays his hands on adults who hurt, and they feel the touch of God in compassion.

To own this three-generational vision of the gift of the Spirit and to multiply power to those who come after us, you and I must first lay claim to the promise that both Jesus and Peter spoke and, second, we must respect the gifts and the capacity of children—and even of new believers—to know, experience and move in the power of the Holy Spirit.

By and large, the Church as a whole has not done this. We have accepted the lie that children are too immature to understand or deal with the experience of the Holy Spirit, and so we have fed them knowledge *about* Jesus without an experience *of* Him. This must change. Every several weeks in our church, for instance, we break the children away from their normal program in another part of the building to bring them into the sanctuary specifically to minister healing to the adults in prayer with laying on of hands. Miracles have followed.

The Holy Spirit does not shrink Himself in order to enter a child. He is the same no matter whom He chooses to indwell. The prophet Samuel was only a small child when he received his first vision from the Lord and responded to His calling. Jeremiah was a *na'ar* (a boy of perhaps fourteen years) in the Hebrew of Jeremiah 1:6–7 when God called him to exercise power over nations in his prophetic ministry. The fires of revival will continue to burn brightly where the Church learns to think three-generationally.

Inter-Generational

Since the vision has always been three-generational through inheritance passed down to natural and spiritual sons and daughters, it must also be *inter*-generational as the young and the old share in the anointing, working and ministering side by side.

Hundreds of years before the coming of Jesus, Joel prophesied:

> "It will come about after this that I will pour out My Spirit on all mankind; and your sons and daughters will prophesy, your old men will dream dreams, your young men will see visions. Even on the male and female servants I will pour out My Spirit in those days."
>
> Joel 2:28–29

How is it that we have so often missed the inter-generational vision embedded in these verses for a revival shared and experienced by every age group simultaneously?

For many years, prophecies have circulated asserting that revival will come through the youth. In the 1980s a prophetic voice dubbed those who were then teenagers "the chosen generation." Now twenty years later much of the generation of young believers who heard those prophecies struggle to keep faith and hope alive, and yet these prophecies persist, applied now to a still younger age group.

Prophecies that revival will come through the youth propagate a lie, a deception authored by a spirit of false prophecy designed to keep the Body of Christ spinning its wheels in frustration. First, such prophecies do not stand the test of Scripture. The Bible consistently paints a picture of the generations *together*. See, once again, Joel 2:28–29 as well as Jeremiah 31, where it says:

"They will come and shout for joy on the height of Zion, and they will be radiant over the bounty of the LORD—over the grain and the new wine and the oil, and over the young of the flock and the herd; and their life will be like a watered garden, and they will never languish again. Then the virgin will rejoice in the dance, and *the young men and the old, together,* for I will turn their mourning into joy and will comfort them and give them joy for their sorrow. I will fill the soul of the priests with abundance, and My people will be satisfied with My goodness," declares the LORD.

verses 12–14, emphasis mine

Second, such false prophecy puts a burden on young people that they cannot carry for lack of strength, seasoning, maturity and wisdom. Having fallen for this deception, in the late 1990s and early 2000s the people of my church made the mistake of laying this burden upon our youth. We believed we were speaking vision and inspiration into them, but it ultimately destroyed our youth group and caused a wounding that held back that generation of young people for years to come.

Third—and perhaps worse—this commonly repeated falsehood sends a message that the older generation has no real calling and plays no significant role in the works of God. Our godless culture exalts youth and devalues age. By contrast, the Bible celebrates the strength and enthusiasm of youth, but honors and exalts the wisdom and position of age and maturity. Proverbs 20:29 provides just one example of many: "The glory of young men is their strength, and the honor of old men is their gray hair." The truth is that we will receive revival in the power of the Holy Spirit as the generations together or we will not receive it at all.

The word given to Malachi, the last prophet of the Old Testament, reads,

Behold, I am going to send you Elijah the prophet before the coming of the great and terrible day of the LORD. He will restore the hearts of the fathers to their children and the

193

hearts of the children to their fathers, so that I will not come and smite the land with a curse.

Malachi 4:5–6

God promises to restore the generations to one another in love. We will be sent into the world together and we will rise up in the Holy Spirit together, having been filled with the power of the Holy Spirit together.

The Power

Jesus taught, "I am the vine, you are the branches; he who abides in Me and I in him, he bears much fruit, for apart from Me you can do nothing" (John 15:5). Clear enough. If we are to become a prophetic people, a source of light to the world, we certainly cannot do it without the Holy Spirit.

Once upon a time I was a good seminary-educated pastor in the charismatic renewal teaching what my education had prepared me to teach. Theologically that meant I believed in the gifts of the Holy Spirit but rejected the idea of the baptism in the Spirit as a second experience after conversion. I had been taught to believe that we receive it all at conversion and I had written brilliant academic papers in seminary to back my position. I left the doctrine of the second experience after conversion to the Pentecostals.

But then I suffered through the long, slow demise of the charismatic renewal. The Third Wave followed after that in the 1980s and ultimately shared the same fate. In 1996 the Toronto Blessing hit me like a freight train, and for several years I asked no questions as I simply enjoyed the powerful works of God that came with that outpouring. It soon became obvious to me, however, that regardless of what they might have called it, all those who went out from Toronto and other centers of renewal to shake the world had experienced something extra—and often extreme—

194

that definitely came after and transcended the conversion experience.

I began to reexamine key passages of Scripture, stripping away much of the intellectual and verbal gymnastics I had studied and in which I had engaged over the years. Fresh truth emerges when you permit the words to simply speak for themselves. I came to the inescapable conclusion that Jesus sent two impartations of the Holy Spirit, each in its own context and each with a distinct and different purpose.

Infilling and Immersion

The first impartation came in John 20:

> So Jesus said to them again, "Peace be with you; as the Father has sent Me, I also send you." And when He had said this, He breathed on them and said to them, "Receive the Holy Spirit. If you forgive the sins of any, their sins have been forgiven them; if you retain the sins of any, they have been retained."
>
> verses 21–23

As the Father had breathed into Adam the breath of life at the beginning, so Jesus breathed the regeneration into His disciples after the resurrection and before He ascended into heaven. In the original Greek, to "retain" means something like "to seize and hurl." With this inbreathing, therefore, came authority to forgive and conquer sin.

Later, in a different time frame and for a different purpose, He promised, "For John baptized with water, but you will be baptized with the Holy Spirit not many days from now" (Acts 1:5), and again, "But you will receive power when the Holy Spirit has come upon you; and you shall be My witnesses both in Jerusalem, and in all Judea and Samaria, and even to the remotest part of the earth" (verse 8).

In John 20 Jesus breathed into them and filled them with the Holy Spirit as authority over sin. In Acts 1, however, Jesus gave them a new promise in three parts, three things they did not receive when He breathed on them or else He would not have told them to wait to receive them.

First He promised them an immersion, more than a filling. The word for *baptism* literally means "immersion." To be breathed into is a very different thing than being immersed. Second, He promised them power of a quality they had not yet received when He breathed on them. Third, He gave them a purpose for the power, that they would go forth to bear effective and miraculous witness to Jesus.

As commanded, they waited and prayed ten days in the Upper Room (the difference between the forty days Jesus spent with them after the resurrection and the Day of Pentecost, fifty days after Passover). When the Holy Spirit fell, they heard a mighty rushing wind filling the house, saw tongues of fire on every head, experienced spiritual drunkenness, spoke with other tongues and bore miraculous witness through the gift of tongues. Out in the street, Peter preached and three thousand gave their lives to Jesus. Continual increase followed (see Acts 2:47). Later, another five thousand men with their families became believers (see Acts 4:4), and all along the way they experienced demonstrations of power in the form of healings and other wonders and signs. These were measurable evidences of the gift of power.

Philip preached in Samaria in Acts 8 and the people believed, but the baptism in the Spirit came as a second experience with dramatic and measurable effects when Peter and John came from Jerusalem to lay hands on them. Dramatic visible effects were in evidence when Cornelius's household received the Holy Spirit while Peter was still speaking (see Acts 10). In Acts 19 Paul found disciples in Ephesus who had not received the Holy Spirit. Something visible and measurable happened to these disciples when they received the baptism in the Holy Spirit.

In each case, the baptism had a dramatic and visible impact on those who received. In each case measurable change resulted in those who were so baptized, and in each case significant increase in the number of believers followed. People began doing things they had never done before and could not have done without the supernatural enabling of the Holy Spirit.

The Necessity of the Demonstration of Power

If we believe that we have been baptized in the Holy Spirit, then where are the signs and wonders? Where are the resurrections from the dead and the miraculous healings that validate the Gospel we preach? Have we experienced the fullness of the promise, or merely hints and dribbles? Or have we experienced anything at all? What Paul wrote still holds true:

> I was with you in weakness and in fear and in much trembling, and my message and my preaching were not in persuasive words of wisdom, but in demonstration of the Spirit and of power, so that your faith would not rest on the wisdom of men, but on the power of God.
>
> 1 Corinthians 2:3–5

And again, "But I will come to you soon, if the Lord wills, and I shall find out, not the words of those who are arrogant but their power. For the kingdom of God does not consist in words but in power" (1 Corinthians 4:19–20).

Our generation will no longer respond to theological propositions and superior words. At the level of our culture, experience has become the new measure of truth. Demonstrations of power are no longer optional. No church will be a lighthouse church that will not pursue anew the baptism of the Spirit, immersion in the power of God for witness that goes beyond mere forgiveness of sin and that carries us into the world to supernaturally demonstrate the sovereignty of God.

Historical Examples

Just three historical examples out of many serve to illustrate the depth of what I long to see. Jonathan Edwards, whose church in Northampton, Massachusetts, received the spark that lit the First Great Awakening in America in 1734–35, witnessed what he called tears, trembling, groans, loud outcries, agonies of body and the failing of bodily strength. From the spark lit in his church, revival swept the colonies until it was said that scarcely a conversation could be held anywhere that did not turn to the things of God.

During the Cane Ridge, Kentucky, camp meetings of 1801, it was said that many people impacted by the Holy Spirit experienced "the jerks," in which they would convulse so violently that hats, bonnets and combs would fly off and women's hair would snap with such energy as to crack aloud like a whip. Thousands of people camped out for days at a time and the meetings often lasted twenty-four hours a day. Hundreds at once would be laid out in the Spirit as if a giant scythe had cut them down. Helpers would carry them out of the meetings to lead them through prayers of repentance and cleansing from sin. The Second Great Awakening followed.

Out of the Great Azusa Street Revival that began in 1906 came many testimonies of healing, as well as similar tales of manifestations and the wonderful, loving presence of God. People flocked from all over the world to experience it and came away changed. Today many hundreds of millions have been impacted by the tsunami waves of life that flowed out from that visitation of the Spirit of God.

Nothing has happened in any renewal during my lifetime to compare with these historic moves of God for power and effect, either in the meetings (although the Toronto Blessing comes close) or on the culture around them, although significant movements have come and gone.

Manifestations of the Spirit

Each of these historic revivals saw massive manifestations of the Holy Spirit, together with untold thousands of conversions. Manifestations caught the attention of the surrounding culture. People came to see what was happening and found themselves captured by the power of it, just as on the original Day of Pentecost. Baptism in the Spirit, indeed!

Having lived through the Jesus Movement, the charismatic renewal, the so-called Third Wave and finally the Toronto Blessing, I conclude that although we in North America have seen hints and dribbles of the power of God, we have yet to experience the true baptism in the Spirit. Obviously, those of us who long for the rise of lighthouse churches and who hunger to make a prophetic impact on the people of the culture around us must long for just such a baptism and lay siege to the gates of heaven until it comes.

Manifestations and Healing

Studying these revivals both in Scripture and in history, I see a connection between manifestations and healing. Manifestations do not cause healing, but it seems undeniable that manifestations and healings accompany one another. Deny one and you will squelch the other. Surrender one and you will surrender the other. Why? Because in denying or suppressing either of these, we deny the power of God in general. The same power seems to produce both effects. On the Day of Pentecost they were visibly drunk in the Spirit and three thousand came to Jesus—two effects produced by the same outpouring. Never in my own experience have I seen healing power significantly released in an environment devoid of the sorts of troubling manifestations of the Spirit that draw the fire of critics today.

For instance, in 1998 during a Sunday evening meeting the Spirit fell with such force that we had removed two rows of chairs to make room for the bodies strewn across the floor in various states of paralysis, semi-consciousness, laughter and convulsions. One of our number had suffered for some time with fibromyalgia, a very painful disease of the muscles. Knocked to the floor by the Holy Spirit in the evening service and unable to do anything but pull herself along on her belly, or crawl, she felt led to take Communion. We practice a perpetual, self-serve Communion with tables set up on either side of the sanctuary. With complete disregard for personal dignity, she crawled to the Communion table, reached up to partake and was instantly healed. No more fibromyalgia! The same power produced both the manifestation and the healing. Squelch one and you squelch the other.

The church in North America largely lost the move of God that began in 1994, first because we spent it on ourselves, and second because we rejected it as too messy. Lighthouse churches must work to be centered in the sacrifice of the cross, building selflessness into the character of the flock and of its people, and they must be ready to absorb and work with the kind of messiness that has come with every powerful visitation of the Holy Spirit from Bible times to the present day.

The Effect

1 Corinthians 12

The Holy Spirit comes with vision and with power. Power has a definite effect.

> Now there are varieties of gifts, but the same Spirit. And there are varieties of ministries, and the same Lord. There are varieties of *effects*, but the same God who works all things in all persons. But to each one is given the manifestation of the Spirit for the common good.
>
> 1 Corinthians 12:4–7, emphasis mine

First Corinthians 12 goes on to speak of healings, miracles and the kind of oneness that causes us to rejoice together over the honor given to other brothers and sisters, a one- ness that leads us to suffer as one when one of us suffers. It speaks of interconnectedness and love. All of these are effects of the power of the Holy Spirit flowing through the gifts He bestows on each one of us. The key is "each one." "To each one is given."

In order for 1 Corinthians 12 to work, we must choose to believe and trust two things. First, we must trust that God has gifted each one according to His Word. Second, we must choose to believe in and trust one another, or rather, the Spirit of God *in* one another. Love "believes all things" (1 Corinthians 13:7). We will never experience the fullness of the Spirit's power without oneness with one another, and we will never have oneness without trust. Further, we will never have trust without forgiveness, patience, selflessness and all the other qualities Paul wrote of in 1 Corinthians 13. Because He is the Spirit of Jesus, He will never lead us out of covenant with one another. He will only lead us into covenant. Covenant bond is a primary effect of the Spirit.

Similarly, He will never lead us into judgment, but only into forgiveness. This, again, is an effect of the power of the Spirit. He will never counsel us not to reconcile, but will only lead us into reconciliation. Effect. Except in cases when sin or relational violation reaches an eleven on a scale of ten and we see no evidence of repentance after due process of loving confrontation, He will never lead us to break relationship. He will only lead us into relationship. Vision, power and effect!

Fruit

Consistently, the Holy Spirit leads us into the fruit of the Spirit, the expression of His nature through us. Fruit equals effect. "But the fruit of the Spirit is love, joy, peace, patience, kindness, goodness, faithfulness, gentleness, self-control; against such things there is no law" (Galatians 5:22–23).

I have already spoken of increase in the context of generational inheritance. "Fruit" also implies increase. Where the

Spirit of God goes, increase follows. The fruit—or effect—of the Spirit is love, joy, peace, patience and kindness *increasing*. I cannot always be kind, but He can through me. I cannot love perfectly, but He can through me.

Let us return to Acts 1:8: "You will receive power when the Holy Spirit has come upon you; and you shall be My witnesses both in Jerusalem, and in all Judea and Samaria, and even to the remotest part of the earth." Fruit means increase in numbers of those being saved. Here is the promise of the gift, the power of the gift and the effect of the gift. Where the power of the Holy Spirit flows and where people receive and apply it as they should, God adds souls, often in exponentially increasing numbers. Effect!

Summary

The baptism in the Spirit enables and empowers us to do things that we could not do in our natural state. Is it not high time we stopped measuring our possibilities and ministries, what we can do with our lives, how we face obstacles and who we can affect for good, by the gifts, abilities, fears and limitations we see in our natural selves?

A prophetic people, a lighthouse church, routinely overcomes limitations of flesh and self by the power of the Holy Spirit. In fact, an expectation of transcendence permeates the very air. Seek this. Pray for this. Expect this. Receive this. Cultivate a hunger for a true baptism in the Spirit. Do this and, as I have so often illustrated, we will see miracles of healing and the transcendent presence of the Lord in our church services, in the workplace, in the public square, in the home and in the neighborhood.

14

Choosing Passion

I could have chosen many topics to finish out this book. The most likely would have been "righteousness," an obvious problem in the current cultural climate, even—and perhaps especially—among Christian leaders. Clearly an essential ingredient for a prophetic lighthouse people! In fact, this topic was my original intent, but the Lord's heart for this book points in a more positive direction. Let us assume holiness as necessary to the radiance of a lighthouse prophetic people and end this book with an emphasis on passion, without which none of what I have written here can work.

The burden for this chapter came as I prepared for Palm Sunday 2008. I had been picking up on a troubling trend in some of the people of my church that boiled down to zeal surrendered and passion lost. In spite of a renewed outpouring of God's Spirit in our midst, some of the faithful were "just going through the motions."

Meanwhile, across a broad front, I had been taking in a lot of really bad news from the world. On March 11, 2008, CNN.com reported that one in four teenage girls in the

U.S. has a sexually transmitted disease and that among African-American girls the rate accelerates to half. During that season my staff and I performed a flurry of weddings for young adults who had come to the Lord under our ministry during their teen years, but for every marriage we performed, it seemed there were one and a half unwed pregnancies affecting families within our congregation. The *Rocky Mountain News* reported that more than one in a hundred Americans is currently incarcerated and stated that the U.S. has more people behind bars than any other nation in the world.

During this same period of time, an angry mother stormed into our youth room after the meeting had ended, grabbed her daughter by the hair (leaving clumps of it on the pool table) and began to drag her out of the building. Instinctively reacting to the pain, the daughter punched her mother, whereupon the conflict became an open fistfight. At that point four police officers arrived to arrest the daughter, who had earlier been reported as a runaway. Although the mother had initiated the physical abuse, the police handcuffed the daughter and hauled her off to a juvenile detention center, charged with assault.

I learned that my state of Colorado is number one in the nation for teen depression. Too frequently our youth staff have been forced to deal with teen suicides and attempts at suicide. Last year one of our local high schools was shut down twice for violence on campus.

Three weeks after the incident with the mother who invaded our youth room, the governor of New York resigned his position because of revelations that he had paid for the services of a call girl. And that was only one incident in an accelerating avalanche of sleaze among national leaders! I wish I could say that our Christian leaders have remained clean in all of this, but as we all know, this has not been the case. In my own region, it seems that pastor after pastor has been exposed in unethical and immoral behavior—everything from financial fraud to sexual trespass and even sexual abuse, sometimes involving minors.

Our culture teeters on the precipice of collapse while the church stands ill prepared to deal with it. Laid-back Christianity has become the order of the day, a cancer eating away at the effectiveness and influence of the Western Church. Jesus said in Revelation 3:15–16, "I know your deeds, that you are neither cold nor hot; I wish that you were cold or hot. So because you are lukewarm, and neither hot nor cold, I will spit you out of My mouth."

In light of all this, for loudly shouting that I intensely hate laid-back Christianity I make no apology. This brand of faith practiced in too many churches and by too many individual believers has proven itself powerless to address the growing problems I cite here. For a very long time laid-back, lukewarm Christianity has dominated the religious landscape of the Western Church, and for our lack of passion we now pay the price in human misery and darkness. I am tired of the compromises, tired of the emptiness, tired of the general weakness of our impact on the world around us, tired of the destruction of precious lives, tired of dealing with the damage, hurt and death that result from wholesale disregard for the laws and principles of God that He designed to ensure life, joy and prosperity.

Yes, we have seen outpourings of God's Spirit in recent decades and I would be the last to minimize their significance, but truth be told, the renewals we saw in Toronto, in Pensacola and in other places impacted only a small minority of the Christian population, and even among those who experienced the touch of these moves of God, much leaked away in the years that followed. For countless believers, passion died and something "less than" took its place. We settled for something smaller than God intended and less than He had given, both morally and spiritually.

So why and how do believers lose their passion? And how do they get it back? A significant part of the answer lies in the depression and despair that result from common misunderstandings concerning the processes we must undergo to attain our God-ordained destiny.

Four Phases on the Road to Destiny

Easter week has always been a great time to examine the life of Jesus. From Palm Sunday to Easter Sunday we remember that extraordinary season when Jesus went from entering Jerusalem in triumph surrounded by joyous crowds waving palm branches and hailing Him as the conquering Messiah, to being put on trial, whipped to within a single stroke of death, crucified, dead, buried and ultimately resurrected.

We must be careful to remember that from the time of His birth until the accomplishment of the empty tomb, the cross remained His goal. He came to save us and there was only one way to do it. His whole life therefore became a determined march toward that terrible destiny. In obedience He determined to be crucified and then to rise from the dead in victory so that we could share His life.

In the same way, God has given each of us a glorious destiny. But instead of appearing instantly and mysteriously out of the ethereal clouds, destiny unfolds over time and through an often difficult process. On the way to that destiny we commonly pass through at least four phases. The same is true of entire congregations as God reveals corporate destiny and then leads the members collectively through the process.

I saw these phases as I studied the lives and ministries of Jesus and the disciples and examined the events of Easter week. If Jesus and the disciples experienced these things, how could we possibly expect to be exempt? Unfortunately, at some point in passing through these phases, many of us find the journey too difficult and so we surrender passion. In doing so, we fall among those of whom Jesus said, "For many are called, but few are chosen" (Matthew 22:14).

Phase One: The First Taste of Excitement

When God first releases an anointing, our purpose seems clear, power flows freely and excitement fills the air. The same held true as the ministry of Jesus began. Matthew described the response of the people as Jesus delivered His first major sermon to a crowd of thousands on a hillside by the Sea of Galilee: "When Jesus had finished these words, the crowds were amazed at His teaching" (Matthew 7:28). Matthew 4 speaks of the early days of His healing ministry in Galilee, saying:

> The news about Him spread throughout all Syria; and they brought to Him all who were ill, those suffering with various diseases and pains, demoniacs, epileptics, paralytics; and He healed them. Large crowds followed Him from Galilee and the Decapolis and Jerusalem and Judea and from beyond the Jordan.
>
> verses 24–25

Like a fire driven by a high wind in a dry forest, the news of His words and deeds raced through the land. Jesus, the wonder boy! Large crowds followed after Him! Heady stuff for a small group of young disciples! Good times! In those early days Jesus' fame grew and everyone thought well of Him. I can see the twelve in a modern setting filled with self-importance and letting everyone know, "I'm on Jesus' ministry team! I'm His right-hand man! I could get you a backstage pass! A private audience!"

Later He sent them out to heal the sick and cast out demons, and then followed up with seventy more. "The seventy returned with joy, saying, 'Lord, even the demons are subject to us in Your name'" (Luke 10:17). Jesus' own heart swelled with exuberance as He saw the power of Satan being broken and people set free: "He said to them, 'I was watching Satan fall from heaven like lightning. Behold, I have given you authority to tread on serpents and scorpions, and over all the power of the enemy, and nothing will injure you'" (verses 18–19).

All revivals and movements of the Holy Spirit begin with joy and excitement. Even as an individual, when you first come to Jesus and His warmth fills you, everything is joy and wonder. The initial impact of the power of the Holy Spirit might cause you to shake, fall or laugh—and again, all seems happiness and excitement.

Clearly, because He knew His purpose and understood what must transpire, Jesus Himself held no expectations that this phase would continue unabated. He had fixed His eyes on the ordeal of the cross that lay before Him, knowing where the ministry would lead and the price He must pay. By contrast, the disciples thought their time with Jesus would be an uninterrupted trip onward and upward. This rendered them completely unprepared for what had to happen—just like you and me.

Many prophetic people spoke glowing words over my congregation when the Holy Spirit began to dramatically impact us in 1996. As word spread of the outpouring at our church, people came from all over the region for our Sunday evening renewal meetings. Like the disciples in Bible times, we really expected our prophetic destiny to unfold in linear fashion, from glory to glory uninterrupted. But then the criticism began to come from outside while from the inside we lost 40 percent of our congregation. Mystified at how anyone could fail to love what God had sent, we could only watch while many we had loved left us in protest against something that frightened them or that they felt was just too messy. Thus phase two begins.

Phase Two: Opposition Forms

For Jesus and the disciples, times of trial began to intrude upon these times of excitement. As He began to communicate troubling truths, people left Him. John reported that "many of His disciples withdrew and were not walking with Him anymore" (John 6:66).

208

Opposition grew among the religious establishment as the Pharisees mounted their attack, questioning the validity of His teaching and challenging the source of His miracles, just as the critics do today whenever revival breaks out. They began looking for ways to trip Him up in His words and eventually plotted to kill Him. As a result, Jesus' own heart ached: "O Jerusalem, Jerusalem, the city that kills the prophets and stones those sent to her! How often I wanted to gather your children together, just as a hen gathers her brood under her wings, and you would not have it!" (Luke 13:34).

At this stage, facing growing opposition, I am not certain the disciples minded much. Certainly the opposition mounted, but Jesus routinely bested the arguments of the Sadducees and Pharisees. Of this the Twelve must have been very proud, and the miracles continued while the crowds of people kept growing!

In the midst of this swirl of activity, Jesus began telling them of His purpose. "From that time Jesus began to show His disciples that He must go to Jerusalem, and suffer many things from the elders and chief priests and scribes, and be killed, and be raised up on the third day" (Matthew 16:21). Although He tried to prepare them for the dark time to come, they had brought into their relationship with Jesus their own vision of where it would all lead. They had signed on for the excitement and for what they believed their dedication to Jesus would mean for them in terms of importance, place and position. A kingdom! Power! Glory!

Make no mistake! In this season, unless blinded by the same things that blinded the disciples, you begin to learn that things will not always be what they were at the start. The journey from that early rush of power and joy to the destiny at the end does not form a straight line. Consequently, in ignorance Jesus' own people began seeking to prevent Him from pursuing His goal. "Peter took Him aside and began to rebuke Him, saying, 'God forbid it, Lord! This shall never happen to You'" (Matthew 16:22), and that was just the start. In the minds of the disciples, destiny could not possibly include suffering, setback, pain or rejection. After the first taste of excitement always comes the opposition designed to turn you away, discourage you and drive you to despair.

Phase Three: The Season of Darkness

Then came the real suffering, first in Gethsemane where Jesus began to absorb our sin, agonizing so intensely over it that He sweated great drops of blood. In this He stood alone because even the three who had been closest to Him could not stay awake long enough to pray in support of what He had to do.

Soldiers came to arrest Him. At His trial false witnesses stood up to accuse Him. The beating and the scourging followed. Peter denied Him. The others ran away. Because they had been deaf to what Jesus told them concerning the necessity of this dark time, they had not counted on the time of darkness. At heart it was a message they did not want to hear.

They had signed up for the first stage, the excitement, the joy and the adoring crowds. They had weathered the opposition phase with relatively undiminished joy and hope because the power remained and because Jesus kept winning all the arguments with the Pharisees, but this was different. Jesus had clearly told them why He had set His heart to go to Jerusalem, but through the filter of what they themselves longed and hoped for, they could not hear it.

Jesus rode into Jerusalem to the shouts of the people hailing Him as a conquering hero. The cry "Hosanna to the Son of David!" means almost exactly, "Save now, O King!" Jesus, the descendant of David, would be their victorious Messiah and King. He would lead them into a golden age of restoration and power. Unprepared for the truth, both the disciples and the people saw in Jesus the fulfillment of their dreams, so when the soldiers came to arrest Him the disciples fled, all except John, who stood with His mother Mary all the way to the cross.

Every believer will at some point suffer intense pressure to flee, to quit, to abandon the quest. At such times you discover that the excitement you experienced at the beginning had a different purpose than the agenda you brought with you. God's purpose is always perfect, a better way to live and serve, but the old purpose, the excitement, the longing for Jesus to fix everything in your life or to grant place or position, blinds you to the revelation of the real thing. The pressure of this time of darkness can lead you to fall away, to choose bitterness or to surrender your passion.

While many in my own congregation have stayed with me through the difficult years, I have lost count of those who once knew the power of the Holy Spirit but have fallen away from church involvement, disappointed and even bitter when the promised destiny failed to unfold quickly enough, or when pressures and obstacles loomed large. Still believers! But broken and disillusioned.

For His part, through it all, Jesus never wavered from the goal He had set for Himself. It was determination, it was passion and it changed the world. Passion is what it takes, but passion must be chosen.

Phase Four: The Final Test

The trial lasted all night. They beat Him, mocked Him and delivered Him to the Romans, who scourged Him within an inch of His life, literally. Not much remained of His physical strength. At the end of His endurance, they forced Him to carry His own cross to the place of His crucifixion. His destiny lay in resurrection, in His rightful place at the right hand of the Father, and for every knee in heaven and on earth to bow before Him, but for the time being, near death, He had yet to carry one more heavy load.

The greatest test, the doorway to *your* destiny, will never come when you feel strong and ready. The most crucial and most difficult test always comes at the point of your greatest weakness, when you feel the most beaten and most discouraged. The decisions you make at that time, the choice of whether to move forward with *passion*—or to just go through the motions or even quit—will determine the shape of your life from that moment forward. These decisions form a fork in the road, one path leading away, and one path representing the way to your God-ordained destiny. Consider Jesus, "who for the joy set before Him endured the cross, despising the shame, and has sat down at the right hand of the throne of God" (Hebrews 12:2).

Every great move of God, or every individual commitment of a life to Jesus for that matter, begins in exuberance and joy, but sooner or later comes the season of the test. Jesus began in exuberance and joy with miracles, crowds of people and the triumphal entry into Jerusalem, but that was never the heart of it. He marched relentlessly and purposefully to the greatest test of His life in His suffering and death. The choices He made at that time ensured His glorious destiny. He did the most difficult thing at the point of His greatest physical and emotional weakness.

Because of these choices, He achieved a resurrection into life that He now shares with us. There could have been no resurrection, no salvation for us and no outpouring of the Holy Spirit in power on the Day of Pentecost had He not chosen to endure the passage through the cross and to do it with passion.

Becoming Great Men and Women

Three kinds of people populate the Church, each of them characterized by the presence or absence of chosen passion: (1) the forgotten ones; (2) the mediocre ones; (3) the great ones. The choices we make with regard to passion will determine which of these we become. The original disciples did not become great men by accident. The time came for them to choose, and choose they did. The same applies to you and me and to the Body of Christ in our time.

The Forgotten Ones

Forgotten men and women sign on for the excitement. Having heard of the works of God and the wonder of His presence, they show up for a while, worship with enthusiasm and talk about how great Jesus is. But then the opposition or difficulty phase appears, the new wears off and they begin to sit with their arms folded, watching passively while others worship.

Never transcending the self-oriented consumer mentality, they fail to catch the vision to serve and so they invest in no one. Because they invest in no one, they really come to love no one; because where your investment lies, there your love will be also (see Matthew 6:21). After a short time we begin to see them less and less until we no longer see them at all. Forgotten, they make no impact on the world for good or ill.

The Mediocre Ones

Mediocre men and women pass through the same process of excitement followed by the same difficulty. Although we see them week after week as they keep faithfully attending, they, too, end up sitting passively at the back of the sanctuary, spectators to the sacrifice of passionate worship others offer, but having lost a passion of their own. They may participate in various ministries, and even be consistent in them, but the intensity has long since died. They simply go through the motions, empty and dry, doing what they do because they know not what else to do, but hope is lost and passion has failed.

The Great Ones

Great men and women experience everything the forgotten and the mediocre experience. The same opposition.

The same heartache. The same erosion of hope. The same disillusionment. The same four stages on the road to destiny. But where the mediocre surrender passion to discouragement, disappointment or depression, great men and women choose it *deliberately*, not on the basis of a feeling or an emotion but because they know they must. In fact, they may have opposite feelings, or even no feelings at all. Jesus' own prayer in Gethsemane teaches us the nature of it. Soulfully and desperately He prayed, "My Father, if it is possible, let this cup pass from Me; yet not as I will, but as You will" (Matthew 26:39). Obviously, Jesus had no desire to go to the cross, but He set His will and chose it with passion for the sake of the glory that would come on the other side, knowing well the despair His decision would bring, that He would be alienated from the presence of His Father for a time. Passion cannot be merely an accidental emotional state, but rather a decision.

Great men and women choose passion in their worship because they know the alternative is death and because they understand the impact of their lives and actions on others. Great men and women choose passion because, like Jesus, they have chosen to live for others' sakes.

Great men and women in my flock have told me quietly how discouraged and disheartened they have felt during certain seasons. Some of them have experienced extended seasons when the presence of God seemed far off, and yet I have seen them worshiping by choice with a consistent and visible passion. They serve, not just consistently and faithfully, but with chosen intensity. Glory comes to such as these. These are the great ones who make a difference in this world.

In the months and years leading up to the world-changing 1906 Azusa Street revival, chosen passion led William Seymour, a black man in a very racial time, to sit outside the auditorium in the hallway as Charles Parham taught white people concerning baptism in the Spirit. Apparently, the idea of entire sanctification as taught by Charles Parham did not include integration. For some time after this, Seymour suffered persecution and criticism because he taught baptism in the Spirit when he himself had not yet experienced it. I do not have to imagine—I know—the discouragement he must have felt, the pain he carried at certain times.

What if he had obeyed that discouragement, given up the passion for what he hungered for and walked away rejected? What if he had given up hope of ever being touched by God in the way for which he hungered, allowed a personal pity party to rob him of his passion and then stopped pressing in to ask God for more? Some eight hundred million people would never have been touched by the power of the Holy Spirit. Uncounted hundreds of thousands would never have come to Jesus in the first place because there would have been no movement of missions flowing out from the great Azusa Street revival.

William Seymour became a great man because he chose to stay with it, not merely to go through the motions but to persevere with passion—chosen passion. All great men and women in history have been like that.

Roots of Discouragement

At the root of most of the discouragement with God and faith that I pick up on in everyday believers is a list of circumstances representing elements of opposition. It might be economics, a job loss or a job search that seems to go nowhere. Or the believer has a job but cannot seem to make enough money. Perhaps a string of disasters has devoured resources and put the believer on the edge financially. Some struggle with the emotional impact of extended physical illness. Others encounter forms of heartbreak as when their children make poor choices or when there is a death in the family. For some it might be that the things they hoped to do in ministry somehow have not yet opened up. Important dreams have never yet materialized. Proverbs 13:12 says, "Hope deferred makes the heart sick." Life just has not turned out as they hoped it would.

Similarly, the people of Jerusalem had a list of circumstances they wanted changed, and on Palm Sunday they hailed Jesus as the One who was supposed to fix them. The Roman occupiers taxed them to death while the Roman occupation army held their nation in bondage, limited their freedom and insulted their God by their very presence. They lived largely in poverty and suffered with illnesses for which they knew no cure. They hoped for the coming of the Messiah who would end all that. His reign would bring power, prosperity, healing and the judgment of the Gentiles.

Jesus' disciples held dreams of glory and power in the Messiah's Kingdom, and yet just hours before His crucifixion He declared, "My kingdom is not of this world" (John 18:36). The truth of His true purpose rather violently dashed their hopes and brought them to utter despair. Ultimately, while the disciples fell into deep darkness of spirit, the people vented their bitter disappointment by crying for His crucifixion.

Jesus' true purpose was to save us for eternity and at the same time shape our character by scouring out the sin that destroys both our own lives and the lives of the people around us. In place of sin, He would implant in us His own nature. By contrast with the desires of the people and even of His own disciples, He suffered death and then rose from the grave in order to deal with the true cause of our unhappiness, discouragement and despair.

Circumstances are never the problem. A real disciple of Jesus can live in joy anywhere anytime because he or she understands his or her purpose and chooses to live it no matter what the circumstances of life might be. This is why Paul could say in Philippians 4:11–13,

216

Not that I speak from want, for I have learned to be content in whatever circumstances I am. I know how to get along with humble means, and I also know how to live in prosperity; in any and every circumstance I have learned the secret of being filled and going hungry, both of having abundance and suffering need. I can do all things through Him who strengthens me.

That is freedom! That is victory, not rooted in circumstances but rather transcending them.

This takes me back to a story I told in chapter 4 from my early days in Denver, when I had been attacked and belittled at the point of every ministry gift in which I had ever placed confidence. I cannot remember a time when I felt so deeply discouraged and hopeless as I did then. I had no friends and had been so slandered by so many lies that I felt I had no options and nowhere to go. Under the weight of all this, I fell into despair and paralysis.

And then that woman with fire in her eyes thrust her head through my office door and said, "Don't let these people defeat you. You're a thoroughbred. Now run like one." God spoke prophetically through her to challenge me to pick myself up and choose the passion that difficult circumstances and unjust opposition had taken from me. Her words awakened my inner warrior and I went to battle. I won. With the power of my Lord, I won.

Every one of you reading this book bears the spiritual genetics that make you a child of God, or you would not be reading these words. You are thoroughbreds. Run like it. Know and use what Jesus has given you. Personally, I intend to become a great man and to lead a great people to make a difference for the Kingdom of God, not because of unhealthy or sinful ambition, but because mediocre people never change their world and mediocre churches make no real impact on the communities around them.

One last passage: "Blessed is a man who perseveres under trial; for once he has been approved, he will receive the crown of life which the Lord has promised to those who love Him" (James 1:12).

Let the lighthouse churches arise. Let them make a prophetic impact on cities and nations. Let us gather the refugees, heal the sick and raise the dead. Let us become all that our Savior called us to be.

About the Author

R. Loren Sandford is the eldest of six children born to John and Paula Sandford, widely recognized as pioneers in the charismatic renewal, prophetic ministry and inner healing. Following a career as a traveling rock musician during his high school years in north Idaho, Loren attended the College of Idaho in Caldwell, Idaho, where he earned a bachelor's degree in music education in 1973. At college in 1972 he met and married his wife, Beth.

Following graduation they moved to Pasadena, California, where Loren attended Fuller Theological Seminary, earning a master of divinity degree in 1976. While there, Loren and Beth served as youth pastors in a Methodist church in La Palma, California, and brought the first two of their three children into the world. Upon graduation Loren accepted a position as youth pastor at Hope United Methodist Church in Sacramento where he served for two and a half years.

In January 1979, Loren accepted the invitation to become co-director of Elijah House in Coeur d'Alene, Idaho, alongside his father, who had founded the ministry several years prior. In that position he helped craft the teachings that later became the Elijah House counseling schools while he did personal counseling and pursued an international teaching ministry.

In August 1980, he felt led to plant Cornerstone Christian Fellowship in Post Falls, Idaho, just six miles from the offices of Elijah House. The family heritage had been in the Congregational Church (later to become the United Church of Christ) where his father pastored for twenty years before founding Elijah House. It seemed a natural thing, therefore, to seek ordination in that historic liberal denomination and to work for renewal from within. Consequently, Cornerstone Christian Fellowship came into existence as a member congregation in the United Church of Christ. Loren later served on the national board of directors for Focus Renewal Ministries, the organization working for charismatic renewal within the UCC, as well as continuing to serve as a board member and teacher with Elijah House.

By 1988 the membership of Cornerstone voted to withdraw from the denomination, citing foundational doctrinal differences, and within a few months had found a home with the Association of Vineyard Churches. Three years later Loren accepted a call to become the executive pastor of the Denver Vineyard, then one of the largest Vineyard churches in the nation.

Through a series of confirming circumstances and events, it became clear that Loren was once again to plant a church. In October 1992, New Song Fellowship was born on the north side of the Denver metroplex, where Loren continues as senior pastor.

In 1996, having been profoundly impacted by the Toronto Blessing, New Song affiliated with Partners in Harvest, the network of churches born out of that revival stream. Since then Loren has often served on the international advisory council for Partners in Harvest. In Denver he has served on many committees working for unity among Christians, including Denver Metro Transformation, Rocky Mountain

Awake, Rocky Mountain Fellowship of Christian Leaders and the March for Jesus.

In Denver Loren has written, produced and recorded eleven music CDs and has authored several books, including *Prophetic Worship, Burnout: Renewal in the Wilderness, Purifying the Prophetic: Breaking Free from the Spirit of Self-fulfillment* and *Understanding Prophetic People: Blessings and Problems with the Prophetic Gift*. From earliest childhood he has been immersed in the move of the Spirit and prophetic ministry. His books reflect a lifetime of experience, gifting and study in the area of prophetic gifting. He and his wife also often host Denver Celebration on KRMT TV, Daystar Television Network. In addition to pastoring the church, Loren has an international teaching and worship ministry.

Married since 1972, he and Beth have two daughters and one son who have collectively given them eight grandchildren. Loren is also a member of the Osage Nation, a Native American heritage he deeply treasures.

More on the Prophetic from Loren Sandford

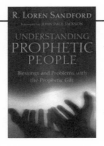

Because prophetic people are often misunderstood—by those with and without the gift—pastor Loren Sandford clarifies the role and office of this extraordinary ministry. Covering an array of topics, including why prophets seem extreme and moody and the four signs of a true prophet, Pastor Sandford calls on prophets to step out of loneliness and on the Body of Christ to step into balance and wholeness.

Understanding Prophetic People by R. Loren Sandford

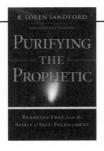

When the Church substitutes genuine spiritual experience for mindless entertainment and caters its prophetic voice to people's perceived needs, prophetic pastor Loren Sandford offers hope and correction. Join those who embrace a vision for cleansing the prophetic stream and who are rediscovering miracles, healings and their firm foundation.

Purifying the Prophetic by R. Loren Sandford